The Long Road to GETTYSBURG

The Long Road

JIM MURPHY

to GETTYSBURG

CLARION BOOKS • NEW YORK

Clarion Books
a Houghton Mifflin Company imprint
215 Park Avenue South, New York, NY 10003

Text copyright © 1992 by Jim Murphy

Book design by Mary Ahern

Maps copyright © 1992 by Jeanyee Wong

Printed in the USA

Library of Congress Cataloging-in-Publication Data

Murphy, Jim, 1947-
The long road to Gettysburg / by Jim Murphy.
p.   cm.
Includes bibliographical references and index.
Summary: Describes the events of the Battle of Gettysburg in 1863
as seen through the eyes of two actual participants, nineteen-year-
old Confederate lieutenant John Dooley and seventeen-year-old Union
soldier Thomas Galway. Also discusses Lincoln's famous speech
delivered at the dedication of the National Cemetery at Gettysburg.
ISBN 0-395-55965-0
1. Gettysburg, Battle of, 1863 — Juvenile literature.   2. Lincoln,
Abraham, 1809-1865.   Gettysburg address — Juvenile literature.
[1. Gettysburg, Battle of, 1863.   2. Lincoln, Abraham, 1809-1865.
Gettysburg address.   3. United States — History — Civil War,
1861-1865 — Campaigns.]   I. Title.
E475.53.M946   1991   90-21881
973.7'349 — dc20   CIP
                                                               AC
HAL 10 9 8 7 6 5 4 3 2 1

To
Jim Giblin — for
his friendship,
encouragement,
and
good advice

~Acknowledgments~

I would like to thank the following individuals and institutions for their generous help in locating research material and photographs.

Patricia H. Chieffo, Associate Curator, Jon K. Reynolds,
University Archivist, and Joseph T. Durkin, S.J., Professor
of American History, Georgetown University.
Terry Parmelee, Picture Department, Smithsonian Magazine.
Mary L. Suggs, Editor, Stackpole Books.
Walter Lane, Lane Photographers Studio, Gettysburg.
Cory Hudgins, The Museum of the Confederacy.
Jerry L. Kearns, The Library of Congress.
The Staff of the Gettysburg National Military Park.

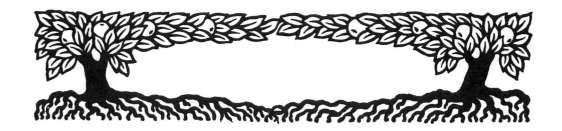

C O N T E N T S

The Long Road to GETTYSBURG

Abraham Lincoln, 1863. Three years of terrible fighting have left President Lincoln tired and strained.

INTRODUCTION

O N the morning of November 19, 1863, twenty thousand people gathered on a gently sloping hill in Gettysburg, Pennsylvania, to witness the dedication of the National Soldiers Cemetery. The ceremony was scheduled to begin at eleven o'clock. Almost an hour later, President Abraham Lincoln still sat, waiting like everyone else. He shifted in his chair to find a comfortable position.

There was no mystery about the cause of the delay. The featured speaker of the day, Edward Everett, was making some last minute changes in his speech.

Everett was a cultured and accomplished man, having been president of Harvard University, then governor of Massachusetts, a United States senator, minister to England, and, finally, secretary of state. Now, at the age of sixty-nine, he was one of America's most famous orators. To prepare for his task at Gettysburg, Everett had devoted a full two months to writing and revising his speech. For an occasion so important and so solemn, the speech had to be perfect — even if the President of the United States waited while additional changes were made.

When the crowd grew restless, the marine band struck up a lively marching tune. At the back of the audience, a photographer set up a large, cumbersome wet-plate camera on a tripod. This was a historic day and he wanted to capture some of it in pictures. Unfortunately, every time he released the shutter, boys started fooling around in front of him, peering directly into the lens and tipping their hats.

Lincoln reached into his coat pocket to touch the two pieces of paper on which he'd written his own speech. He wasn't impatient or angry with the delay. He respected Everett and admired the painstaking care the older man was lavishing on his oration.

If anything, Lincoln might have been a bit apprehensive. Just seventeen days before, on November 2, he'd been asked to make "a few appropriate remarks." With the Civil War still raging in the South, Lincoln's presidential duties allowed him little time to write a speech, even a very short one. In fact, he'd only finished it the night before in the room where he was staying.

The curious peer into the camera while behind them the crowd waits for the dedication ceremony to begin.
The double image below was made to give the photograph a three-dimensional effect through a viewer called a stereoscope.

An even more important reason Lincoln may have been apprehensive was that he was in a vulnerable position politically. The three-year-old war had already taken tens of thousands of lives and there was no sign that it would be over soon. Many people — including some Lincoln supporters — were beginning to wonder whether Lincoln's goals of ending slavery and keeping the Confederate states a part of the Union were worth the cost. "Our bleeding, bankrupt, almost dying country longs for peace," the famous journalist Horace Greeley wrote to Lincoln. "I entreat you to submit overtures for pacification to the Southern insurgents."

But Lincoln knew that the South would never stop fighting unless he agreed to preserve (in the words of the Confederate Constitution) "the rights of the States unimpaired" — and this meant their right to have slaves. Lincoln would simply not go along with such a compromise.

Still, the movement toward peace at any cost was growing more and more popular. Already, rivals were preparing for the presidential elections that were to be held in 1864. And one way to "prepare" was to discredit Lincoln in the eyes of voters. Right now, in the crowd in front of Lincoln, were several newspaper reporters who were eager to make headlines out of any mistake he might make.

Of course, Lincoln could have refused the invitation to speak. With the war still going on and his son, Todd, gravely ill back in the White House, no one would have blamed Lincoln if he'd declined to attend. The truth was that he had wanted to be a part of the ceremony — he needed to see the landscape of Gettysburg where so many men had died.

Suddenly, there was a murmuring from the crowd and then scattered applause. Everett had finally arrived.

A path was cleared through the crowd and Everett made his way to the platform and his seat. As quickly as possible, the ceremony was begun. First, the chaplain of the House of Representatives offered a prayer, followed by music from the band. Then Everett rose to give his speech.

Everett was more than a highly skilled speaker; he was a master showman as well. He had memorized every sentence of his thirteen-thousand-word speech, then rehearsed them over and over for dramatic effect. Even his hand movements were faultless. In a high, clear voice he began: "Standing beneath this serene sky, overlooking these broad fields now reposing from the labors of the waning year, the mighty Alleghenies dimly towering before us, the graves of our brethren beneath our feet, it is with hesitation that I raise my poor voice to break the eloquent silence of God and Nature. But the duty to which you have called me must be performed; — grant me, I pray you, indulgence and your sympathy."

Edward Everett.

With this seventy-three word warm-up, Everett launched into the main body of his speech.

Lincoln had been given an advance copy of Everett's speech, so he was familiar with its contents. Even so, he must have been impressed by Everett's scholarly references to ancient Greece and its warrior gods, and the powerful way in which he spoke. Lincoln may have even compared his own little speech to the grand one Everett was delivering. It's also very probable that Lincoln's thoughts eventually strayed to the reason for the gathering at Gettysburg that day.

Less than five months before, in July of 1863, the Union and Confederate armies had met there in a bloody three-day battle. The hill where twenty thousand stood listening to Everett had been the scene of the most brutal fighting of the war. When the cannon and gun fire had stopped, six thousand Confederate and Union soldiers lay dead and an incredible forty-two thousand were left wounded.

As President and Commander-in-Chief, Lincoln was legally responsible for the actions of his army. Lincoln's involvement went much deeper, however. From the moment the first shots had been fired at Fort Sumter back in 1861, Lincoln had played an active part in the way the war was fought. He'd formulated policy, drawn up strategic plans, and he'd even directed the movement of troops. Lincoln was a daily visitor at the War Department where he spent hours reading the telegraph dispatches pouring in from officers at the battlefields — and fired instructions back on the spot.

Lincoln believed firmly that the only way the United States would be restored was the complete defeat of the Confederate army. To bring this about, he'd constantly urged his commanders to take on the Rebel army in a head-to-head fight. Major battles had taken place — Shiloh, Bull Run, and Antietam, to name a few — but none had been decisive, mainly because the Union generals had failed to be aggressive. Then in early June a telegraph message had arrived at the War Department. The Confederate army was on the move, it reported, and seemed likely to invade the North.

On hearing of the possible invasion, Lincoln called a meeting with the commander of the Union forces, Major General Joseph Hooker, and his senior staff officers. During this conference, Lincoln said to them: "Gentlemen, in your next battle *put in all your men.*"

Lincoln's order had been carried out in the rocky hills, ravines, and woods that now surrounded him. He had known all along that a major clash of the two armies would cost many lives, but the long rows of white grave markers were vivid proof of just how steep the price had been.

Lieutenant John Dooley.

1

WE ARE MARCHING

THE sun had barely risen on June 3, 1863, and already the seventy-five thousand men of the Confederate army were up. Many grumbled about the early hour as they splashed water in their faces, had a cup of strong black coffee, and packed their gear. They'd been told to prepare for several days of travel, but didn't know why they were marching. Among them was a nineteen-year-old lieutenant named John Dooley.

Dooley moved among his men, urging them to shake the sleep from their eyes and get ready. He wasn't a forceful leader, being shy and soft-spoken by nature. And at 5 feet 8 inches tall and 130 pounds, he was frail compared to many of the brawny Virginia farm boys under his command. Still, his men respected him for his fairness and intelligence and soon they were lined up on the road.

Dooley, like many Southern officers, had brought along one of his family's slaves to cook, wash, and run errands. Since this promised to be a long and very hard march, Dooley decided to send his servant, Ned Haines, back home to Richmond where he would be safe. After doing this, Dooley took out the pocket journal he carried throughout the war. While waiting in the road next to his men, he managed to scribble, "This morning we are marching towards Tappahannock." Then the order to march was shouted up and down the long line of soldiers and Dooley and his men moved forward.

No major highway connected their camp near Richmond with the little town of Tappahannock, so the army traveled along a series of narrow and rutted dirt roads. Their route took them through farmland that had been the scene of recent savage fighting.

"Scarce a farmyard that is not stained by human blood," Dooley wrote during a brief halt in the march. "Scarce a field unpolluted by the enemy's touch. The fences are burned, the meadows trampled down, the cattle all gone and the harvests unharvested; proud homesteads in ruins. . . ."

Dooley was a peaceful and gentle person by nature, but the sight of the ravaged countryside angered him immensely. This was the work of the Northern invaders, that "party of brutal men, uneducated, unrefined, unprincipled, inhuman, and criminal." His opinions might seem extreme, but they were typical of how many, if not most, Southerners felt. In addition to defending their homes, Southerners like Dooley were also trying to preserve their way of life — and this included the right to hold slaves.

In addition to Ned Haines, Dooley's family owned a number of other slaves. Dooley was fond of all his family's servants and treated them as fairly and as kindly as possible. Yet, the condescending nature of Dooley's true feelings came through clearly when he wrote, "Ned, like all negroes, would not like to labor for his living." As far as Dooley was concerned, blacks needed to have their lives strictly regulated in order to survive, which, in his eyes anyway, justified slavery. "The southern people," Dooley said proudly, "understanding the characters and disposition of the negroes, gave them their proper place in Society."

It was the burning, almost fanatical desire to defend the South and all it stood for that kept Dooley and other Southern soldiers fighting despite the great odds against them. From the very start of the Civil War, the Confederate army had been vastly outnumbered

A tough, no-nonsense bunch of Confederate soldiers hauling cannons up a pass in the Blue Ridge Mountains.

General Robert E. Lee (center), surrounded by some of his most trusted generals.

by the Union forces and short of food and rifles. Yet time and again the South had managed to come away victorious — at the Battle of Bull Run, at Wilson's Creek, at Shiloh, and at Fredericksburg. Just weeks before at Chancellorsville, a tired and scattered Confederate army had outmaneuvered and confused the Union forces and their commander, Major General Joseph Hooker. What had been a sure Union victory turned into an embarrassing retreat. No wonder Dooley could survey the long line of Confederate soldiers that stretched ahead and behind him and say, "Never before has the army been in such fine condition, so well disciplined and under such complete control. Perhaps never before have we had a larger effective force, sixty thousand infantry with some two hundred pieces of cannon. There are also from seven to ten thousand cavalry."

Credit for the success of the Confederate army had to go to its commander, Robert E. Lee, and his staff of imaginative senior officers. Together, they had devised a strategy of locating the weak spot in the enemy's forces, striking it quickly, and then pulling out before a counterattack could be launched. It was Lee and his officers who inspired the men and kept fighting units intact during battle. Of course, credit had to be shared with Southern soldiers. They were a tough, hardened bunch of fighters who obeyed the orders of their officers without question. More important, and unlike Union soldiers, they had the habit of victory.

After several days of marching, the Confederate army headed northwest, following roads that took them through the town of Culpeper Court House. Temperatures during the day rose to 95 degrees and the boots of thousands of soldiers ground the road into a fine dust.

"Terrible [was] the march along the scorched and blazing plains of Virginia," Dooley recalled. "Choking, blinding were the clouds of dust that rose from beneath the army's unsteady tread. The heat is frightful, and the road in many places is strewn with the sun-struck."

One of Dooley's men staggered and nearly fell under the weight of his gear. After giving him water, Dooley shouldered the man's heavy rifle and let the man carry his sword instead. The rest of his men were also weary and their feet dragged through the dirt and gravel of the road. Even the feisty company dog hung its head and walked along listlessly. Despite the heat, none of Dooley's men dropped out. "Such days as these prove the true soldier," Dooley wrote with pride, "and he who falters not in the long and wearisome march will not be absent from the charge."

Twenty-one days after starting, new orders were issued and Dooley at last learned something about where they were headed. "We are moving in the direction of Martinsburg and learn for the first time that Pennsylvania is our objective."

The flat terrain changed outside of Culpeper as the army entered the foothills of the Blue Ridge Mountains. To get through the small mountain passes and narrow dirt roads, the army had to divide itself up into smaller units. This would leave them open to attack until they were out of the mountains and able to regroup, but Lee wasn't worried. He was certain they had not been detected by the enemy.

Invading the North was a gamble, but Lee did not see any other option. The Confederate victory at Chancellorsville had driven Hooker's army off, but had not destroyed it. Lee knew that the Union would soon regroup and launch another, even bigger attack, and he wasn't at all certain his army could win a second time.

Lee saw several advantages to taking the war north. First, the lush farmlands of Pennsylvania had not been destroyed by the war. There would be large supplies of meat and grain available for his troops and plenty of fodder for the horses. Second, moving the Confederate army north would confuse and worry Hooker. Hooker

General Robert E. Lee. Among his troops he was referred to affectionately as "Uncle Robert."

would assume that Lee was planning to attack Washington and fall back across the Potomac to defend the capital. Every Union commander — from Winfield Scott, to George McClellan, to Ambrose Burnside and now Hooker — had shown themselves to be conservative and predictable fighters, preferring to defend safe positions

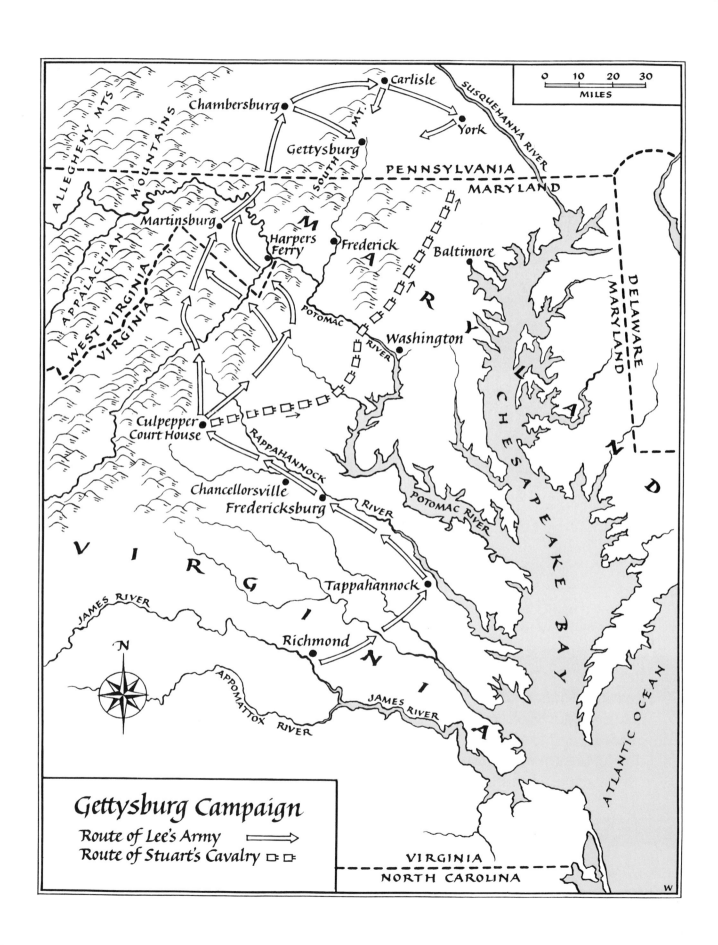

CHAMBERSBURG

Carlisle

SUSQUEHANNA RIVER

ALLEGHENY MTS

MOUNTAINS

Chambersburg

Gettysburg

SOUTH MT.

York

PENNSYLVANIA

MARYLAND

0 10 20 30
MILES

Martinsburg

Harpers
Ferry

Frederick

Baltimore

APPALACHIAN MOUNTAINS

WEST VIRGINIA

VIRGINIA

POTOMAC

M
A
R
Y
L
A
N
D

DELAWARE

MARYLAND

RIVER

Washington

Culpepper
Court House

RAPPAHANNOCK

POTOMAC RIVER

CHESAPEAKE BAY

Chancellorsville

Fredericksburg

RIVER

V I R G I

JAMES RIVER

N

Tappahannock

ATLANTIC OCEAN

Richmond

N I A

APPOMATTOX RIVER

JAMES RIVER

Gettysburg Campaign

Route of Lee's Army

Route of Stuart's Cavalry

VIRGINIA

NORTH CAROLINA

W

rather than attack. There was no reason to think Hooker would act any differently than he had in the past.

Lee had no intention of going after Washington. He planned to threaten Philadelphia and Baltimore instead, and cut Washington off from the rest of the country. This, Lee hoped, would force Hooker to do something he wouldn't normally do — bring his troops out into the open and fight. If this happened, Lee wanted to choose the battlefield, one perfectly suited to his army's style of fighting. A defeat of the Union army might not win the war outright, but it could result in political pressure on Lincoln to negotiate a peace favorable to the South.

There were disadvantages to the plan, and many of Lee's officers opposed the invasion as too risky. The loudest opposition came

Lieutenant General James Longstreet opposed the plan to invade the North and would brood about it throughout the campaign.

from one of Lee's most trusted commanders, Lieutenant General James Longstreet. Longstreet was a solid, dependable fighter and loyal to Robert E. Lee, but he had grave doubts about fighting a major battle in unfamiliar territory. He voiced his opposition openly and tried to persuade other staff members to side with him.

Lee accepted such disunity as a grandfather might a quarrelsome family. Despite the anger and clash of opinions, his "family" of officers would pull together when called upon in time of battle. They had never failed him, even when he had asked them and their troops to do seemingly impossible things.

There was one problem which could not be solved by staff loyalty or spirit alone. At Chancellorsville, his most brilliant general, Stonewall Jackson, had been shot and killed while leading his troops. Jackson was an aggressive soldier who personally had found ways to turn losing battles into miraculous victories. Maybe even more important, Jackson had been a model and inspiration for every Confederate soldier. Wherever Stonewall went there was always the possibility of victory. It was no wonder that when John Dooley

Lee and Stonewall Jackson (right) conferring before the Battle of Chancellorsville. Lee entered Pennsylvania without his best general's advice and leadership.

heard the news of the general's death, he had asked, "Who will fill great Stonewall Jackson's place, who indeed can ever replace our noble hero, so pure, so truly great?"

It was a question that everyone, including Robert E. Lee, was still asking. Lee knew that no one person in his army could replace Stonewall Jackson. He hoped instead that the combined fighting spirit of his officers and men and the predictability of the Union officers would give him the advantage.

On June 25, while his army was marching through Martinsburg, Lee sent Major General James E. B. ("Jeb") Stuart and his cavalry off on an important mission. They were to distract and harass the Union army as much as possible so Lee could get his troops into Pennsylvania unobserved. Stuart was also ordered to gather information on the size and exact location of the enemy. This information was so vital that Lee made it clear he wanted Stuart to return with it in just a few days when they had fully entered enemy territory.

Jeb Stuart was a highly skilled cavalry leader, maybe second only to Stonewall. He was also a flamboyant character who loved to see his name in newspaper headlines, and he viewed this assignment as a great opportunity. He and his men rode off into the Virginia countryside, a thundering mass of horses. In addition to scouting out the enemy and distracting him, Stuart intended to ride completely around Hooker's army. This would be a spectacular feat and would also bring shame on the Yankees.

John Dooley knew nothing at all about Lee's strategies, Longstreet's objections, or Jeb Stuart's bold plans. As a lieutenant, his job was to keep his men organized and marching north. And he and his men were finding the narrow mountain passes doubly hard to march through because a chilly rain had begun to fall. The weather matched the reception they received after leaving Confederate territory.

"Pass through Martinsburg about 11 A.M. and perceive at once that we are not treading friendly streets," Dooley noted. "We found the people very sullen and maliciously disposed, and not a few curses were hurled at us from garret windows; and many young but frowning brows and pouting lips we saw in doorways and on the sidewalks. But our boys laughed cheerfully, and when contempt and scorn were shown them answered by jests and witticisms."

Major General James Ewell Brown ("Jeb") Stuart strikes a dashing pose.

THE ENEMY IS APPROACHING!

I MUST RELY UPON THE PEOPLE FOR THE

DEFENCE of the STATE!

AND HAVE Called THE MILITIA for that PURPOSE!

A. G. CURTIN, Governor of Pennsylvania.

THE TERM OF SERVICE WILL ONLY BE WHILE THE DANGER OF THE STATE IS IMMINENT.

When the Rebel army was finally discovered, a panicky governor sent out these handbills.

The Confederate army had cause to be cheerful. They had entered enemy territory virtually unnoticed. The army had become separated and strung out over forty-five miles of road, but now the terrain was a little less rugged. When they reached level ground, they would be able to consolidate forces and carry out their plan.

The one hitch in the otherwise smooth operation was that Stuart had not returned or sent any messages. In effect, Lee was as ignorant of the whereabouts of the Union army as they were of his. This didn't worry Lee much. He assumed that Stuart's silence meant that the Union army had not followed him.

On June 28, Lee learned otherwise. Word reached him that

the Union army had begun moving and was only about thirty-five miles away. The information did not come from Stuart; a Confederate soldier had blundered on a large force of blue coats and come running. The soldier's report seemed accurate, so Lee decided to pull his forces together as quickly as possible. The various parts of his army would meet where the roads they were on happened to intersect.

Meanwhile, Dooley was impressed to find Pennsylvania lush and unscarred by cannon fire. "The wheat fields are every where nearly ripe for harvesting, and all around plenty appears to bless the fertile land." After gathering some supplies to feed the hungry army, the men found themselves marching down a twisting road that would eventually lead them to a sleepy little town called Gettysburg.

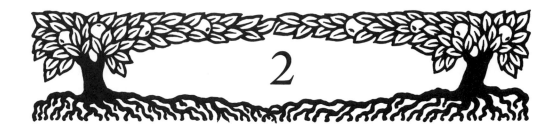

RUMORS AND A LONG MARCH

CORPORAL Thomas Galway had heard the rumors for several days — the Confederate army was on the move again. The trouble was that no one seemed to know exactly where the main body of the Rebel army was or where it was headed. So seventeen-year-old Galway and the rest of the Union army had to sit by the roadside and wait.

With nothing to do, an impatient Galway spent his time playing cards, preparing his meals, and asking passersby for news. A few people reported sightings of Confederate cavalry to the east. Others thought the Rebels were headed toward Washington. A soldier from another brigade said he'd heard that the enemy was headed north, toward the Blue Ridge Mountains and Pennsylvania.

Like many soldiers in the Union army, Galway was eager to fight the enemy. Galway was not very tall, maybe 5 feet 4 inches tall at best, but he had a strong, outgoing personality and did not let anyone push him around. What's more, he was quick to take offense whenever he encountered prejudice, something he'd experienced firsthand. Many times while searching for a job in his hometown of Cleveland he'd come across signs that read "Niggers and Irish need not apply." For Galway, this was a very personal war.

The South — and slavery — had to be defeated and the sooner the better. Finally, on the afternoon of June 14, orders to march were issued.

"At last," an enthusiastic Galway wrote in his diary, "the army is moving once more."

Galway's relief would soon turn to frustration. His company was assigned to be the rear guard for the army, a task they considered tedious and not very glamorous. It also meant that they would have to wait where they were for almost eight hours until the other troops and the supply wagons got under way.

Even when they finally began marching, things didn't go smoothly. "We marched only about five miles tonight although, owing to the frequent halts and changes of direction, it took a good part of the night to march even that distance."

Corporal
Thomas Galway.

Galway had managed to get only an hour of sleep when the bugle sounded the call to wake. Grumpy and groggy, Galway and the rest of the men in his company managed to gulp down some coffee before they were on the road again. Making the march even more arduous, Union forces had to stop every few miles to deal with Confederate cavalry.

"Several times during the day we had to halt and deploy in line of battle columns, the artillery toiling up and down the hill to take position. Having taken position, we would remain until our cavalry had reconnoitered the enemy, when we would again form column and continue the march. All this consumes a great deal of time besides harassing and fatiguing horses and men."

Jeb Stuart had broken his large force of Confederate cavalry into small units and had them probing and poking and bothering the Union Army as much as possible. This they did with such great skill that for nearly two weeks Galway's company spent half of every day dealing with them. The weather didn't help either. Early on in the march, Galway noted that "the sun pours down upon us unmercifully." Ten days after this entry, rain began to fall and the temperature dropped. This would have been good marching weather, except that they entered rough, hilly terrain. "Owing to [these conditions] there is a good deal of straggling."

Straggling simply meant that a soldier was unable to continue marching, so he dropped out of the line to rest. Most stragglers were either tired to the point of exhaustion or injured and in great pain. Even so, straggling was considered a sign of weakness or, worse, laziness. Imagine how embarrassed Galway was when he had to admit, "My feet are very sore. Generally, I am one of the best marchers in our company which, by the way, is considered one of the best marching companies in the brigade. . . . I kept with my company for another couple of hours. Finally I could not put one

The Union army crosses the hilly countryside near the Rappahannock River.

Stragglers chat and boil coffee while a line of fellow soldiers passes by in the night.

foot before another. I was utterly done out, so telling my sergeant of my intentions, I stepped out from the ranks and lay down on a spot of grass."

Later, Galway joined up with a number of other stragglers and settled in for the night. As he slept, a drama that had been developing for several weeks between the commander of the Union army and the President of the United States came to a conclusion.

When Hooker first heard that the Confederates had pulled out of Richmond, he had sent word to Lincoln that he wanted to capture that city immediately. Lincoln rejected this plan and made it clear what he wanted. "I think *Lee's* Army, and not *Richmond,* is your true objective point," Lincoln told Hooker in a wire. "If he comes toward the Upper Potomac, follow on his flank . . . [and] fight him when opportunity offers."

Having his plan turned down did not please Hooker. He was a nervous and excitable man and felt his ability to lead the army was being questioned. For several days after this, he was reluctant to issue commands or make decisions on troop movements, which accounted for the many delays and changes in direction. To Lincoln, Hooker's "slows" began to smell like another defeat in the works. In a meeting with his secretary of navy, Lincoln revealed his misgivings. "We cannot help beating them, if we have the right

Major General Joseph Hooker. Hooker's hurt feelings would eventually lead him to quarrel with Lincoln.

man. . . . Hooker may commit the same fault as McClellan and lose his chance."

Hooker did manage to get his army across the Potomac when he got into another argument with Lincoln. Hooker refused to attack Lee unless he received more troops. Getting more troops to the area would take time, during which Lee might escape again. The request was denied. This angered Hooker enough that on June 27 he asked to be relieved of his command.

Hooker knew full well that this put Lincoln in an awkward position. The enemy had invaded the North and might very well be headed for Washington. To remove Hooker was to invite chaos in the Union army and possibly bring on a major defeat. On the other hand, if Lincoln asked Hooker to stay on as commander, Hooker would demand that Lincoln leave him completely alone. Lincoln recalled the recent defeat at Chancellorsville and bristled at the thought of a repeat of that humiliation. He simply did not trust that Hooker would not get cold feet again. Before the day ended, Lincoln accepted Hooker's resignation.

The next morning, Galway awoke before dawn. "I got up and cooked my coffee, and then went on in pursuit of my regiment." He rejoined them at eight o'clock just as they were about to resume marching. "We reached the heights at Monacacy Bridge near Frederick about two in the afternoon. There I heard that General Meade had taken command of the army." While Galway did feel the timing for the change was bad, like "swapping horses when crossing a stream," he also admitted that "many of our senior officers are said to have lost confidence in Hooker after his failure at Chancellorsville, so maybe the change is good."

Indeed, the army itself had changed long before this and needed new and more daring leadership. The bumbling and inept soldiers who could be routed easily by a Confederate charge had become

Map, facing page:

Once the Union command learned where Lee was headed, the army made a dash to head him off.

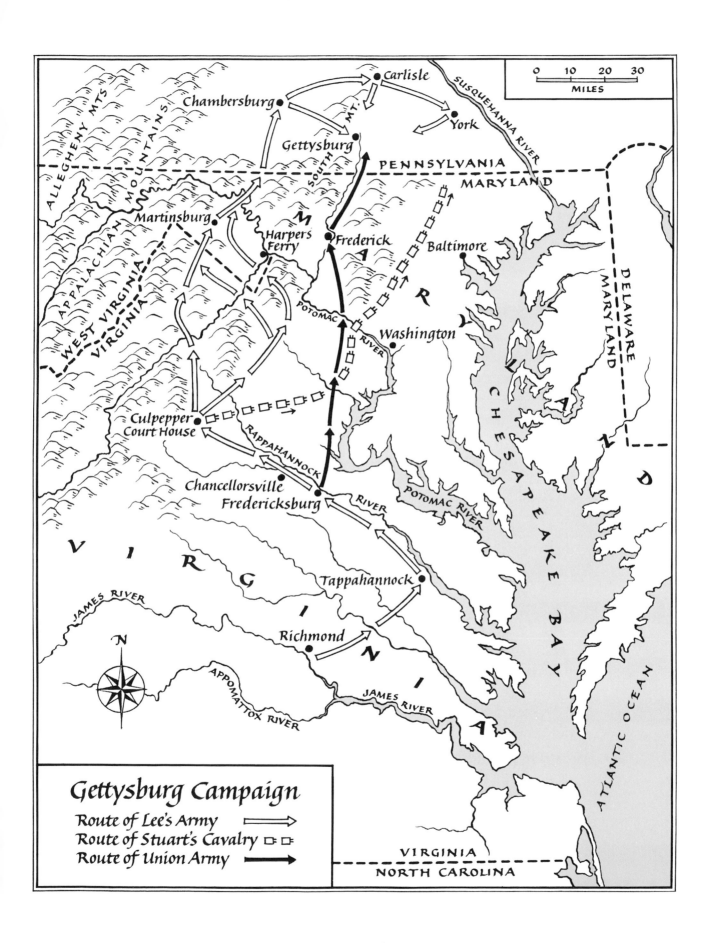

Carlisle

Chambersburg

Gettysburg

York

SUSQUEHANNA RIVER

0   10   20   30
MILES

ALLEGHENY MTS

APPALACHIAN MOUNTAINS

SOUTH MT.

PENNSYLVANIA

MARYLAND

Martinsburg

Harpers Ferry

Frederick

Baltimore

M
A
R
Y
L
A
N
D

DELAWARE
MARYLAND

WEST VIRGINIA
VIRGINIA

POTOMAC

Washington

RIVER

CHESAPEAKE BAY

Culpepper
Court House

RAPPAHANNOCK

POTOMAC RIVER

Chancellorsville
Fredericksburg

RIVER

V   I   R   G   I   N   I   A

Tappahannock

N

Richmond

JAMES RIVER

APPOMATTOX RIVER

JAMES RIVER

ATLANTIC OCEAN

Gettysburg Campaign

Route of Lee's Army
Route of Stuart's Cavalry
Route of Union Army

VIRGINIA
NORTH CAROLINA

*Major General
George Meade.
He would prove
just the sort of
"goggle-eyed
snapping turtle"
the Union army
needed.*

seasoned fighters. They were eager to take on the main body of the Rebel army and in George Gordon Meade they had a general who would allow this to happen.

Meade was an army regular, tough and crusty and quick to lose his temper. Soldiers who served under him referred to him as a "damned goggle-eyed snapping turtle." He was also a man who never backed away from a fight.

Luck was with Meade when he took command. Jeb Stuart had been able to fulfill only one of his two orders. He had managed to confuse the Union army spectacularly. On June 29, Galway was still noting, "We are under arms and ready to march at five in the morning. Then these orders are countermanded. There seems to be doubt as to the enemy's movements. His cavalry are maneuvering so as to cover the real designs of his main column. . . ."

But the second part of his orders — that he report the position of the Union army to Lee — Stuart had failed to obey. It wasn't that he didn't try. Stuart made several attempts to get back, but Meade's army of ninety-five thousand men was so large that it clogged all the river crossings and jammed the local roads. No matter

Cavalrymen traveled as light as possible so they could move quickly from place to place.

The Cavalry skirmish line.

where he went, Stuart couldn't find a fast route around them. As far as the location of the enemy went, Meade and Lee were in the same position.

Instead of blundering along and waiting for something to happen, Meade decided to act. He reasoned that if he found a sizeable part of the Confederate army and attacked it, Lee would pull the rest of his troops in and fight. So Meade sent out Major General John Buford and a force of about twenty-five hundred men to scout the area. In case Buford located a large portion of the Rebel army, Meade had Major General John F. Reynolds trail him with one third of the Union forces.

Like most soldiers, Galway had little idea of what was going on at headquarters or in the field. He was much more concerned with the wet weather, the hilly terrain they were marching through, and his run-ins with Confederate troops. At one point, Galway was put in charge of a small group of men and ordered to scout the area for enemy soldiers.

William J. Jackson
Serg.t Maj 12.th N.Y.Vol.
Sketched at Stoneman's Switch
near Fredricksburg. Va
Jan 27.th /63

*Sergeant Major
William Jackson
of the 12th New
York Volunteers.
His division
would be among
the first to enter
the fighting at
Gettysburg.*

". . . We descended a hill into a valley, the far side of which was wooded, as well as the opposite slopes. I was following the turnpike, according to my instructions. A little way ahead and to the left of the road stood a good sized brick house. As we approached, two women and several young children came running out of the house. This looked suspicious to me. . . . I kept on, meanwhile, but more slowly."

Galway and his men inched forward quietly, tense and ready to fire on the enemy. Instead of a fierce fight, Galway's encounter with the enemy turned out to be something very tame. When he came around the corner of the building, he surprised twenty Rebels who had stopped to eat lunch. He concludes his story matter-of-factly. "I captured a small party of Confederate cavalry who had dismounted and were taking it easy at a clump of trees on the roadside. General Hancock rode up to me after the occurrence and told me that I had done well."

Galway did not have much time to enjoy his victory. Meade had decided that his army was too scattered. He wanted to pull his troops together into a stronger unit and to accomplish this he ordered them on a forced march. Galway's feet did not fail him this time, so it was with a touch of pride that he wrote, "From Monacacy Bridge, to where my regiment bivouacked that night is thirty-one miles. A very good march to make over such roads, and with such packs as we carried."

When they finally made camp, Galway's company was tired but in remarkably good spirits. They had spent over two weeks marching through rough terrain, being harassed by the enemy almost every step of the way. Yet no one in their regiment had been injured, and the army was within a day or so of being completely united and ready to fight.

Hundreds of camp fires dotted the hillside with men gathered closely around them. The rain had stopped, but the night was surprisingly chilly considering it was late in June. Earlier in the evening, their lieutenant had told them of reports that the Confederate army was somewhere nearby and that Meade had scouts out searching for them. When they located the enemy, the lieutenant said, there was going to be a fight. A big fight.

A few of the men laughed this off as nothing but another rumor. Galway and most of his fellow soldiers sensed something different. "Everything became terrifically quiet. For the quiet that precedes a great battle has something of the terrible in it. Everyone knows that there must be fought a bloody battle and all are therefore anxious to save our strength for the contest. Hence the extraordinary quiet."

3

I WILL FIGHT HIM INCH BY INCH

JOHN Buford rode his horse up the hill and into Gettysburg Cemetery, stopping next to a stone wall. From Cemetery Hill, Buford had a panoramic view of the small town and the fields and ridges and roads surrounding it. His attention was focused on the Seminary, a stately red brick building just about a mile to his left. The road close by the building was filled with the gray uniforms of the enemy.

At first, Buford thought he was seeing an isolated raiding party out looking for food and supplies. Then he counted six company flags and realized he'd come across something very different. This

was a lead brigade of infantry, and if he wasn't mistaken, the rest of the Confederate army was not far behind it.

One of the Rebel soldiers spotted Buford's men at the foot of Cemetery Hill. He raised his rifle and fired, but the range was too long so this first shot at Gettysburg fell harmlessly into an empty field. A few moments later, the Confederates halted, did an abrupt about face, and marched back up the road away from Gettysburg.

Why the Confederate troops did not attack puzzled Buford. He could only assume that they had gone back to get reinforcements so they could return in full force. Immediately, Buford sent a messenger back to Meade and Reynolds to tell them he'd found Lee's army and that it was headed toward Gettysburg. Then Buford surveyed the area. If there was going to be a fight, then the best place to be was in the hills overlooking the open fields.

Buford's orders had not specified that he fight the enemy, only that he locate them and report back. With only twenty-five hundred men and a few small cannons, fighting would be a daunting task. Still, Buford was a smart soldier. He knew that given the chance Lee would seize the high ground for himself and force the Union army literally to fight an uphill battle. Buford also knew the fierce tenacity of his men. Not long before, at Thorofare Gap, Virginia,

As Confederate troops came down the Chambersburg pike (shown at right), this was their view of Gettysburg and the surrounding land.

he had held off a force of twenty-five thousand Rebels for six hours with just three thousand men. He couldn't hope to win here, but if he could hold the Confederate army back until Reynolds arrived the Union might have a chance for victory.

Buford sent a small force of men to occupy the town and to watch the other roads leading into Gettysburg. Then he ordered the rest of his men to take positions on the ridge near the Seminary. Dig in deep, he advised them. "They will attack you in the morning and they will come booming — skirmishers three-deep. You will have to fight like the devil until supports arrive."

Major General John Buford. His decision to place his men in strong defensive positions probably meant the difference between defeat and victory for the Union.

THE NEXT MORNING, July 1, before the sun had fully risen, the Confederate army was up and ready. Word had been passed up and down the column of soldiers that the Yankees had been spotted and that there would be fighting before the day was over. John Dooley got his men organized quickly, only to learn that they wouldn't be moving for several hours. "Our Division (Major General George E. Pickett's) is the rearmost," Dooley reported glumly. "We are left to cover the march of the main body advancing on Gettysburg [and] to protect the convoys of horses, cattle, etc., the spoils of our invasion. . . ."

After Rebel soldiers drove off his cows, seventy-year-old John Burns grabbed his flintlock rifle and joined the fight. He was the only citizen of Gettysburg to do so.

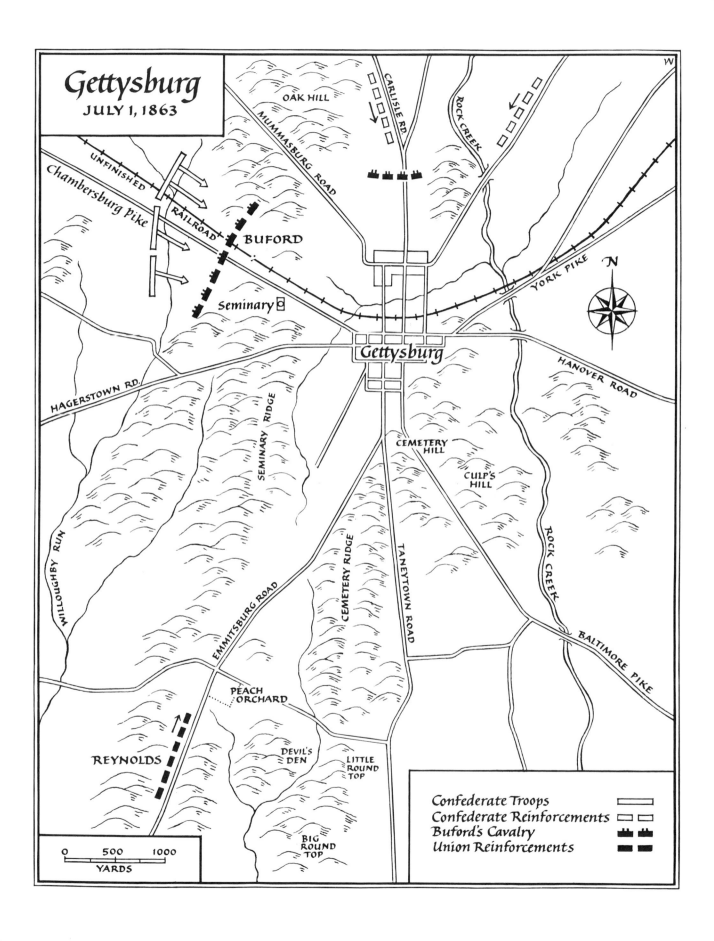

Disappointed that they wouldn't see immediate action, Dooley and his men waited in a clearing near the road and watched as thousands of other soldiers marched past. It was here that Dooley learned he and the rest of the regiment of fifteen thousand men were being held back because Jeb Stuart had not yet returned. He was so angry about this that his pencil tore at the page when he wrote the following: "The cavalry who should be with us but who, under the command of their dashing general [Stuart], are far away towards Washington City, leaving our infantry and artillery unguarded in flank and rear, and stripping our cautious Lee of sufficient force to explore the exact position of his enemy."

AN HOUR LATER and twenty miles away, Thomas Galway grabbed a quick cup of coffee and a biscuit before shouldering his rifle. "We are on the road at seven," he recorded in his journal. "Our advance guard has come up with the enemy, according to messengers coming rearward. Our march is steady but slow. After marching five miles we come to Taneytown [and] are formed into line of battle columns. Then we go on again."

Galway was still five miles from Gettysburg when he heard the sounds of battle. "Heavier and heavier grows the boom of the artillery ahead somewhere." At this point, a buzz went through the troops in anticipation of the fight. "This time we'll show those Rebs," Galway heard some men mumble. "This will be different from Chancellorsville." Then abruptly, the column was ordered to halt and wait by the road until called up. Galway would spend the rest of the day listening to the distant rumble of cannons.

This cannon fire was a small part of the first day's fighting at Gettysburg. As Buford had predicted, the Confederate forces came marching back down the road, this time prepared to fight. Buford's

Map, facing page:

Buford made his initial stand just outside of Gettysburg. Eventually, Union troops would withdraw to new positions along Cemetery Ridge, and on Cemetery Hill and Culp's Hill.

men were widely scattered throughout the hills, some behind stone walls, others using trees and large rocks as cover. His cannon were placed on high ground with a clear view of the road. When the enemy came up the hill, Union soldiers would pop out from cover, aim and fire, then duck back down to reload. Cannon fire ripped apart the Rebel lines easily. From their strong position, Buford's men were able to beat back the initial Rebel charge.

The Confederates weren't about to give up. They moved in artillery of their own and opened fire at the ridge. As this shelling went on, a wave of Confederate infantry began a second advance.

The bullets were flying so thick now that the trees were stripped of their leaves and a thick acrid smoke clung to the hillside. Buford's men hung on despite increasing casualties, but it was clear that the Confederates were inching their way closer and closer. It wouldn't be long before they would overpower the Union soldiers and seize the high ground.

At this critical point in the fight, Reynolds arrived with reinforcements. After a very fast briefing from Buford, Reynolds sent five thousand men into the fight and ordered the rest of his forces to Gettysburg as quickly as possible. Among the troops with Rey-

A Confederate private from Louisiana, Charles Comes, was among the first soldiers killed.

*Major General
John F. Reynolds
brought
reinforcements in
the nick of time,
then fell to a
sharpshooter's
bullet.*

nolds were eighteen hundred men of the famed Iron Brigade, some
of the Union's most seasoned and tenacious fighters. Then Reynolds
sent word back to Meade, telling him that they had engaged the
Confederate army at Gettysburg and urging him to bring up the
rest of the troops. He added that while the enemy was advancing
in force, "I will fight him inch by inch, and if driven into town I
will barricade the streets and hold him back as long as possible."

These were virtually the last words Reynolds wrote. Fifteen
minutes later, while studying the battle line, a Rebel sharpshooter

got him in his sights and shot him dead. Major General Abner Doubleday took temporary command of the Union forces and as he did over three thousand fresh Confederate soldiers came marching down the road from Carlisle. They had a clear shot at the weak right flank of the Union, and would have routed them easily except for a bit of bad luck. Before the Confederate troops could be organized for the attack an additional five thousand Union reinforcements arrived.

Fighting was at close quarters along most of the ridge, with men using bayonets or the butts of their rifles. Artillery from both sides still blasted away at enemy strongholds, often hitting their own men in the confusion and blinding smoke. Neither side pulled back an inch and the casualties mounted. By mid-afternoon, the Iron Brigade had been shattered, with one regiment losing almost 80 percent of its men.

After each enemy charge, Union soldiers had to reform their lines and await the next attack.

Another five thousand Confederates arrived and immediately joined the fight. This new assault was simply too much for the tired and outnumbered Union troops. Lines of battle began to break and soon the army was in full retreat, pulling back along the road and through town. Fortunately, Union artillery had been stationed on Cemetery Hill and along the ridges running south of the town. After savage fighting in town, Union soldiers fled to the safety of the hills and tried to regroup.

General Lee had arrived on the scene earlier in the day, so he had a clear view of what was happening. Oddly, he did not feel confident that he could whip the enemy that day. Only half of the Confederate army was at Gettysburg just then and Lee still had no idea where the rest of the Union army was. It was possible that Meade and the rest of his army were only a mile or two away. If Lee ordered a full attack, he might be sending his troops into a fatal trap. So despite the fact that his men had control of the fight, he issued orders to pull back for the night.

IT WAS a little past five in the afternoon when Galway and his company were ordered to march toward the battle. "Once again we go forward," Thomas Galway wrote. "The sound of the artillery grows more and more distinct. Later in the afternoon we encounter couriers from the front, who give us a little news. Nearly all report desperate fighting near Gettysburg. . . . But at dusk comes the report that the Eleventh Corps, mainly Germans, have skedaddled from the field."

Regiments comprised of Germans were often held up as examples of fine, well-disciplined soldiers, while some considered Irish regiments inferior fighters. For Galway and his Irish friends, hearing that Germans had broken in the heart of battle gave them great joy.

Then about a mile outside of Gettysburg Galway's company came face to face with some members of the Eleventh. Galway doesn't bother to hide his scorn for these men. "But to return to our mutton, to our flying sheep of the Eleventh Corps. We could see them as night came on, gathered in little crowds about their fires, boiling coffee and babbling German. All talking at once; without officers, without organization of any sort; a mere herd of stragglers."

Words were exchanged between the Irish and German units and a fight very nearly broke out. Fortunately, provost guards happened upon the scene and drove the straggling members of the Eleventh forward, back into position.

With the dead all around them and smoke rising to blur their vision, Union soldiers scramble to reload as Confederate troops move closer.

MEANWHILE, John Dooley was as annoyed and as cranky as Galway. Like Galway, he'd heard the rumble of the cannon and received reports about the fierce fighting, but he saw no action at all. Instead, he was assigned the task of "urging forward stragglers and keeping up in fact all who desert their ranks."

After spending most of the afternoon doing this, Dooley's company was moved closer to the fighting. "Between five and six o'clock in the evening we come within sight of the town of Gettysburg, and are marched into a small copse of woods to the right of the road. Here we must bivouac for the night."

In effect, the fighting was over for the day. Lee had pushed the Union forces off the ridges around the Seminary and forced them to retreat. Of the eighteen thousand soldiers used by the Union army that day, over nine thousand had either been killed or wounded or taken captive. Lee was on the verge of another great victory, but he continued to be cautious and decided to consolidate his forces and prepare for the next day's fighting.

SEVERAL HOURS LATER, Galway and his company moved into the hills and took up position. "We arrived at the rear of the battle a couple of hours after dark. Everything is comparatively quiet; not a shot did we hear. Yet there was the lumbering roll of the artillery moving up to available positions for the morning and the loud shouts of men losing one another in the dark."

Because the photographic process used in the 1860s required a long exposure time, Civil War photographers were not able to shoot the battle action. Still they captured all of the grim horror of what took place. Here a Confederate soldier lies dead where he fell.

Meade came on the scene around midnight and conferred with his officers. In the past, Union commanders in a similar situation would have withdrawn from the field to minimize losses. Meade knew that to retreat was to admit defeat and this would weaken Lincoln's position politically and open up Washington and Baltimore to attack. More important, Meade saw that his soldiers held strong defensive positions in the hills and he knew that before dawn a major portion of his army — seventy-five thousand troops in all — would be in the area. Retreat was out of the question, Meade decided. If the Union army was going to fight, then this was the best place for it to happen.

Reporters from The New York Herald *were already on the scene and sending reports back to eager readers at home.*

For the rest of the night as infantry units arrived they were ordered into position in the hills and told to prepare for attack. Galway's company was moved once and then repositioned very late at night as Meade sought to create the strongest possible defensive wall. Galway's concerns were much more basic. "What would an American soldier do without his coffee?" he mused. "Deprive him of his hardtack, of his beans, and his pork, and even of his whiskey. But you must not fail to halt him within reach of water and give him a supply of coffee and time to make a fire to cook it. Then he will be quite content."

Galway sipped his hot coffee as Union artillery and soldiers were being positioned on the heights to rain a killing fire down upon the enemy. Word was passed through the darkness. There would be no retreat. The Union army would either hold the ground or die trying.

4

LIGHTNING BEFORE
THE STORM

Facing page, top:

July 2 began with a fierce cannon duel before dawn.

Bottom:

Typically, eight men and an officer were assigned to each cannon. Most of the men were there to help reposition the heavy weapon during battle.

*T*HOMAS Galway had barely closed his eyes to sleep when the ground shook him awake. The blasts of exploding shells echoed throughout the woods and cannon smoke clung to the ground like a layer of fog. "On Thursday July 2 we are up at four. The artillery on both sides have begun to fire already. Daylight shows us a little stream where we find water to wash ourselves and to make coffee. We are only allowed a few minutes for this, when we fall in and march off."

Galway's regiment was positioned on Cemetery Ridge about three hundred yards to the left of Cemetery Hill. Even with the cannons roaring in the background, Galway took time to detail what he could see. "It is a pretty sight. We can see for miles around to the right and left. Away to the west are South Mountains, beyond which is Chambersburg. At our feet is a pretty valley about two miles wide, bounded on the far side by a low wooded ridge where we can plainly [see] the enemy's line. In the middle of the valley to our right lies the pleasant town of Gettysburg."

There was scattered fighting all during the morning and into the afternoon. At around two o'clock, the fighting grew more intense a mile and half away from where Galway was. "A peach orchard

· 54 ·

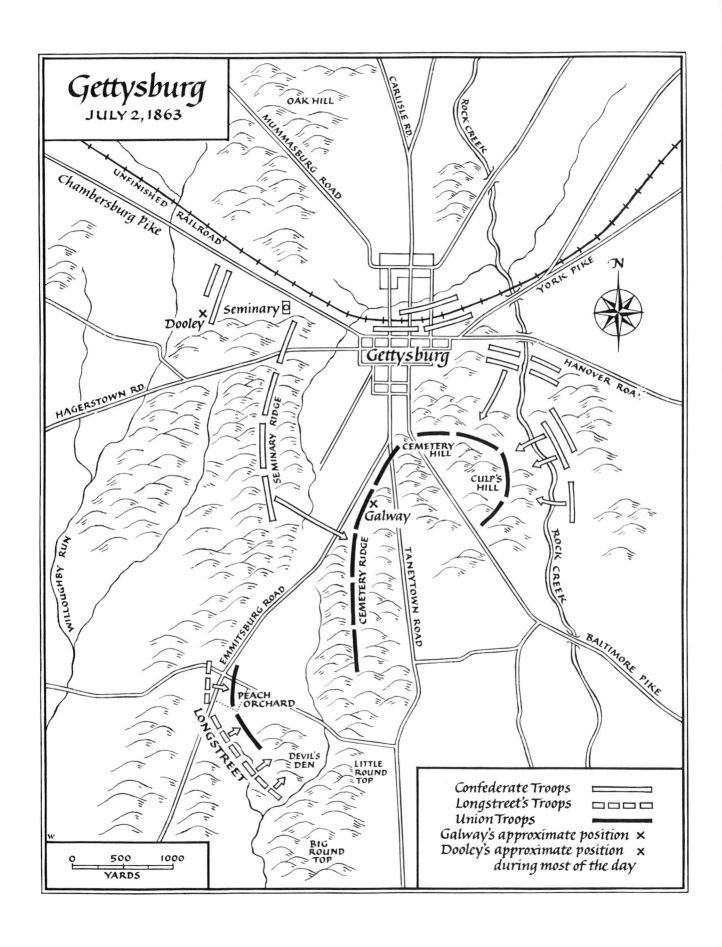

Gettysburg
JULY 2, 1863

OAK HILL

CARLISLE RD.

ROCK CREEK

MUMMASBURG ROAD

Chambersburg Pike

UNFINISHED RAILROAD

YORK PIKE

N

Seminary

× Dooley

HAGERSTOWN RD.

Gettysburg

HANOVER ROAD

SEMINARY RIDGE

CEMETERY HILL

CULP'S HILL

WILLOUGHBY RUN

× Galway

CEMETERY RIDGE

TANEYTOWN ROAD

ROCK CREEK

EMMITSBURG ROAD

BALTIMORE PIKE

PEACH ORCHARD

LONGSTREET

DEVIL'S DEN

LITTLE ROUND TOP

BIG ROUND TOP

W

Confederate Troops	
Longstreet's Troops	
Union Troops	
Galway's approximate position	×
Dooley's approximate position	×
during most of the day	

0   500   1000
YARDS

and a clump of farm houses near the Emmitsburg turnpike was shrouded in the thick white smoke. From the foot of Round Top Hill our artillery is now at work, and it has become a very desperate battle out there. From our position we can see it all very plainly."

Lee had decided to attack both flanks of the Union battle line, hoping to push them off the high ground and complete the rout begun the day before. Longstreet argued against the plan. Circle around the enemy, he insisted, and strike at Meade's rear. Lee turned down his idea. Jeb Stuart had still not returned, so Lee had no idea where the main body of the Union army was. To circle around blindly would leave him open to an ambush. "No," Lee said, pointing toward the ridge. "The enemy is there and I am going to fight him there."

Longstreet's troops were assigned the task of attacking the Union's left flank, then situated in the peach orchard. Another gen-

Map, facing page:

Lee's plan called for Longstreet's forces to secure Little Round Top and then hit the Union's exposed left flank. At the same time another charge would be launched on Culp's Hill.

Only a few Union soldiers offer resistance as Longstreet's charge gets under way.

eral was to go after the right flank which was dug in around Culp's Hill. Both would attack at the same time just as soon as Longstreet had his men in place.

It took until mid-afternoon for Longstreet to move his twelve thousand men through woods and across fields and get them positioned. After the battle, however, many Southerners felt that he had dragged his feet because he was annoyed that his plan had been rejected. Whatever the reason, once Longstreet was ready, he struck the Union line with deadly force. At about the same time, almost ten thousand Confederate troops hit the right flank.

Fighting in the peach orchard raged for several hours, but eventually Longstreet's troops got the upper hand. The Union commander on the left had his leg shattered and was carried from the field. His troops were hardened veterans, so despite the absence of their commander they gave up ground slowly. To the right of the main action, Confederate troops moved into a steep, rocky area known as the Devil's Den, and headed for Little Round Top. If they secured that height, the entire two-mile length of the Union's left flank would be open to enemy artillery fire.

Major General G. K. Warren's quick thinking saved the Union from defeat on the second day.

After being hurried into position, Union artillery launched deadly fire from Little Round Top.

Once again, good luck and timing were on Meade's side. Earlier in the day, Meade had sent one of his best officers, Major General G. K. Warren, to observe the fighting. When Warren rode up, the first thing he saw was a line of Confederate soldiers coming out of the trees and splashing across the creek at the foot of the Little Round Top.

Warren didn't waste time wondering what to do or trying to get permission from superior officers. He galloped off and almost instantly happened upon a brigade of men then moving forward. After ordering them to the top of the hill, Warren went looking for some artillery. This took more time, but he succeeded in finding two cannon crews, located a route up the steep slope, and was able to get them into position in time to hold off the Confederate soldiers.

Fighting on the right flank was just as fierce. The Confederate troops tried to storm Culp's Hill once, then again, and again and again. Each time they were driven off. Still, the Rebel forces kept coming through the murky powder smoke and blistering enemy fire. It wasn't until late in the afternoon that Meade was able to send a fresh brigade to the scene and finally pushed back the Confederate forces.

Action in the center where Galway was stationed was light, though Confederate infantry did probe everywhere along the Union line of battle looking for a weak spot. Most Rebel advances were stopped by Union infantry well before they reached Galway. "While we are waiting," Galway jotted down, "some of us are writing letters to our loved ones, which might be found in our haversacks if we lose our lives in this coming battle."

Late in the afternoon, a large force of Confederate troops were seen moving toward the Union center and Galway's company was ordered to stop them. This was what Galway had been waiting for, and his next entry seems charged with excitement. "We moved down the hill in line of battle in fine style, our colors flying and the artillery as well as the rest of our brigade cheering us. We were deployed to advance into the corn [and] this soon woke up the Johnnies. Now the bullets flew. The batteries on the hill behind us gave us good help, exploding their shells right in front of our skirmishers, but amongst the Confederates. We drove them back from the turnpike and across the fields to a fence and a group of farm houses, where they turned about and checked our further advance."

As acrid smoke rises from the woods on Culp's Hill, Union soldiers, secure behind a log fortification, fire on the advancing enemy.

JOHN DOOLEY'S VIEW of the second day's fighting was a lot less exciting than Galway's. He spent most of the morning in a thick grove of trees waiting for orders. He couldn't see any of the action himself, though he could hear cannon and rifle fire. Then, around noon, he and his men were ordered forward.

"How long we take to gain our positions, what delays, what suspense! We are soon passing over the battlefield of yesterday, and the details of burying parties are digging graves to receive the freshly fallen comrades, and, in many instances, they have only the ghastly and mangled remnants of their gallant friends to deposit in these hastily dug pits. I pass very close to a headless body; the boy's head being torn off by a shell is lying around in bloody fragments on the ground."

Dooley and his company finally stopped an hour later at the foot of a ridge, three quarters of a mile from where Thomas Galway was. There they rested, cooked a meal, played with their dog, and waited for their turn to enter the battle. The order never came. Instead, the afternoon crept by slowly, with Dooley nervously listening to the sounds of battle and trying to guess what was hap-

While Union artillery fires at a distant foe, lines of soldiers keep their heads down, waiting their turn in battle.

pening. "The second day's fighting is now at its height," Dooley wrote late in the day, "and we can hear distinctly the roar of the cannon to our front and to the right of the town. It is a stubborn and bloody conflict."

What Dooley would learn later was that the Confederate strike at the right and left flanks of the Union line had been stopped. Both sides would exchange fire for the rest of the night, and sometimes the shooting would get quite hot, but there would be no real change in position. So Dooley sat out the second day's fighting, wondering when or if his chance would come. Before going to sleep, he made his last journal entry for the day. It was short, but prophetic: "We are sure if we escape tonight, tomorrow we will have our full share."

As the second day of battle wore on, soldiers began to nickname the places where they fought . . . .

ON THE OTHER HAND, Galway spent most of the night at the foot of the ridge, very close to the line of battle. At times, he was less than three hundred feet from the enemy. "We on the skirmish line lay very close to the ground because though it was dark we yet could make out the enemy figures, just as they could see ours."

Once in a while an over-eager soldier on one side or the other would shoot at a shadow he thought might be the enemy. For the most part exhaustion produced an uneasy truce. "My orders were to preserve the utmost vigilance amongst my men," Galway remembered, "an order difficult to execute as we were all exhausted and, moreover, I could scarcely keep my eyes open during the watch. . . . Two or three times it seemed to me that I dozed off, and

. . . This rocky area came to be known as Slaughter Pen.

I would rouse myself and whisper to one of my men who would appear to be nodding. At any rate the enemy must have been as sleepy as me, for he remained quiet too, dreaming perhaps of the happy fields of the South, as they had known them before war called them away." A few moments later, his journal still open on his lap, Galway found he could not keep his eyes open and he fell into a fitful sleep.

When horses were killed or wounded, the job of moving ammunition caissons fell to the soldiers.

As BOTH Dooley and Galway slept, two councils of war were being held that would determine the third day of fighting at Gettysburg. In one camp, George Meade was being advised of the situation. Union losses were estimated to be twenty thousand men killed,

wounded, or captured. Meade knew they were in a dangerous position, and yet he had no intention of withdrawing. Union forces had fought well and still held very strong defensive positions. He studied the map and tried to figure out where Lee would strike next. Since Lee had failed to destroy either of the Union's flanks, Meade reasoned that left him only one spot in the Union line to attack. Meade pointed to the field map. Lee would hit here, he predicted, in the center where Cemetery Ridge joined Cemetery Hill. To greet Lee, Meade ordered even more men and cannon to be placed on Cemetery Ridge.

In Lee's tent, the discussion was more heated. Longstreet advised pulling back to find better fighting ground. Once again Lee rejected Longstreet's plan. A withdrawal was the same as defeat, Lee insisted. Besides, they had come too close to destroying the enemy on both days to leave the job undone. With Jeb Stuart, who had finally arrived on the scene, and Pickett's division, Lee had enough fresh soldiers for one more massive assault on the Union center.

AT AROUND one o'clock in the morning Thomas Galway was startled awake by a flurry of artillery fire. "As we lay on our backs courting sleep, we could at any time see the skies crossed with a network of the fiery traces of shells going and coming, like shooting stars, between the artillery of both sides. Shortly afterwards it became quiet, terrifically so considering the storm which we all knew had been brewing for the morrow."

PICKETT'S CHARGE

THE next morning, July 3, John Dooley and Thomas Galway were both up very early and ready to be moved to new positions on the battlefield. Dooley's regiment marched along a road for a quarter of a mile. "As we turn from the main road to the right," Dooley wrote, "Gen. Lee, better known as Uncle Robert, silent and motionless, awaits our passing by, and anxiously does he gaze upon the only division of his army whose numbers have not been thinned by the terrible fires of Gettysburg."

Like other Confederate soldiers, Dooley loved Robert E. Lee unquestioningly, and seeing him that morning thrilled and inspired him. He was not some general who directed action from the rear safely out of range of cannon fire and sharpshooters. He was there, near the line of battle, with them. "As we pass him the admiring throngs doff their warworn hats and greet his presence with reiterated shouts and most enthusiastic waves." Then Dooley added a bit sadly, "I must confess that the Genl's face does not look as bright as tho' he were certain of success. But yet it is impossible for us to be otherwise than victorious and we press forward with beating hearts."

Dooley then marched across a field where he and his men halted and waited. What would happen next, Dooley wondered. How long would they have to wait? All around them they heard other companies being ordered into position, the thunder of cavalry moving along the road, and the rumble of artillery being hauled up rocky hills. Almost fifteen thousand men would take part in Pickett's charge and they had to be moved from various spots around Gettysburg and then placed very carefully for the assault. In addition, one hundred thirty cannon had to be brought over the rough terrain and then lined up hub to hub just west of the Emmitsburg road. Several hours after stopping a new order arrived and Dooley's unit moved forward.

"A little further we take temporary position in the hollow of a field. Before us is a rising slope which hides the Yankee position from view." Because it was already late in the morning and the sun was beating down fiercely, they were told to relax in the shade. "Around us are some trees with very small green apples; and while we are resting here we amuse ourselves by pelting each other with green apples. So frivolous men can be even in the hour of death."

ON THE OTHER SIDE of the battle line, Thomas Galway and his men were moved across the Emmitsburg road to the most advanced skirmish line. This left them isolated some two hundred yards from the rest of the Union army.

The scene is deceptively calm during the early morning of July 3. To the left a group of sleepy Union soldiers prepare for their day's work.

"All this drew a brisk fire from the enemy, which continued ceaselessly from then out. The rails of the fence had been torn away from the posts and laid upon one another, making a sort of protection for the heads of the men lying down behind them. Well, when we reached the fence we saw what work Death had done. . . . Our dead lay so thick where they had been killed that it was difficult for us to find a place to stretch ourselves."

For the rest of the morning, Galway's company traded fire with the enemy. A hundred and fifty yards to his left, a barn being used by Confederate sharpshooters was captured and set on fire by soldiers from New Jersey. Rebel artillery opened fire on these soldiers and eventually drove them back to the fence.

Rebel sharpshooters picked away at this advance line of Union

Not much time has passed, but the scene has changed dramatically. Cannons have been rolled into position at the right and troops are being moved to Cemetery Hill.

soldiers all morning. The only break in the firing came at around eleven o'clock. Suddenly, Galway was surprised when a Rebel sharpshooter who had been in a tree not more then ninety feet from him began shouting, "Don't fire, Yanks!"

"We all got up to see what was coming. A man with his gun slung over his shoulder came out from the tree. Several of our fellows aimed at him but the others checked them, to see what would follow. The man had a canteen in his hand and, when he had come halfway to us, we saw him (God bless him) kneel down and give a drink to one of our wounded who lay there beyond us. Of course we cheered the Reb, and someone shouted, 'Bully for you! Johnny!' Whilst this had been going on, we had all risen to our feet. The enemy too, having ceased to fire, were also standing. As soon as the

*Lee gallops
among his
troops at
Chancellorsville,
encouraging
them to hold the
line.*

sharpshooter had finished his generous work, he turned around and went back to the tree, and then at the top of his voice shouted, 'Down Yanks, we're going to fire!' And down we lay again and the shooting resumed."

A HUNDRED YARDS AWAY from this scene, Dooley's company was moved again. "Soon we are ordered to ascend the rising slope and pull down a fence, and this begins to look like work. Orders come to us to lie down in line of battle [and we learn] that all of the cannon on our side will open fire at a given signal, will continue for an hour. . . . [Then] we are to charge straight ahead over the open field and sweep from our path any thing in the shape of a Yankee." As a way to orient their advance, Confederate troops were told to march toward a little clump of trees that happened to be at the very center of the Union line.

Behind Dooley, in the field he'd just left, Generals Lee, Longstreet, and Pickett met to go over the details of the charge one last time. In addition to the massive charge, two other assaults were planned in an effort to distract and confuse the Union forces. One would be launched at Culp's Hill; meanwhile, Stuart's cavalry would circle around and bother the Union rear. It was a good plan on paper and, with luck, might work. After Pickett went off, Longstreet tried once again to talk Lee out of the uphill fight. "No fifteen thousand men ever arrayed for battle can take that position," Longstreet later claimed he said. Lee's answer was simple and direct. "They will break," he replied, still convinced that Union soldiers would panic in the heat of battle.

Longstreet rode off to rejoin his staff. Since he was Pickett's superior officer, it was Longstreet's responsibility to give the order for the charge. Because he had no faith that the charge would succeed, Longstreet immediately transferred this duty to the officer directing the Confederate artillery fire. "My heart was heavy," a sad Longstreet would write later. "I could see the desperate and hopeless nature of the charge and the hopeless slaughter it would cause." After this, he grew quiet and seemed reluctant to issue orders.

At that point, Dooley's only concern was making sure his men had loaded their rifles and were ready to move forward when the order came. "Remember," he would tell them several times, "keep moving toward the clump of trees." He also had the company dog tied securely to a tree so it wouldn't follow them into battle. Then he turned and studied the terrain they would be crossing — a grassy meadow almost a thousand yards wide. They would be in the open and easy targets for cannon and rifle fire every step of the way. In

Incidental action before the charge. Here Confederate troops try to retake a stone barn.

Major General George Pickett's eyes have a haunted look about them. Pickett would lead fifteen thousand men in the biggest and most deadly charge of the Civil War.

the distance, Dooley could see Union troops massed along the Emmitsburg road and in the ridge leading to Cemetery Hill preparing to greet anyone who managed to survive the long run.

AT ABOUT THE SAME TIME, a tired and nervous Meade was on the ridge studying the enemy lines with his field glasses. Aside from a spattering of light rifle fire now and then, a haunted quiet had settled over the battlefield. It didn't fool Meade at all. He could see the line of Confederate cannons facing him and hundreds of gray uniforms positioned and ready to charge. A newspaper reporter with Meade realized they were within range of the Confederate cannons and suggested that they move to the other side of the ridge. After ordering more men into the center, Meade rode off to have a quick lunch and wait.

The minutes ticked by slowly, the soldiers tense and anxious. Then "at ten minutes to one precisely," Thomas Galway remembered, "a heavy gun was heard from the enemy's line. A pause of a few seconds followed, when there broke out on the still air a terrific cannonade. From ten minutes to one until half past two this cannonade made those Pennsylvania hills vibrate again with its awful sound. We lay on our backs in the ditch, our heads to the enemy. We could see our artillerymen with their jackets off and their sleeves rolled up, at work at their guns."

Map, facing page:

Pickett's charge would sweep past Galway's vulnerable position to strike at the Union center.

JOHN DOOLEY remembered that the sound of the signal had barely stopped echoing when cannon fire from both sides opened up. "The earth seems unsteady beneath this furious cannonading, and the air might be said to be agitated by the wings of death. Over 400 guns nearly every minute being discharged!"

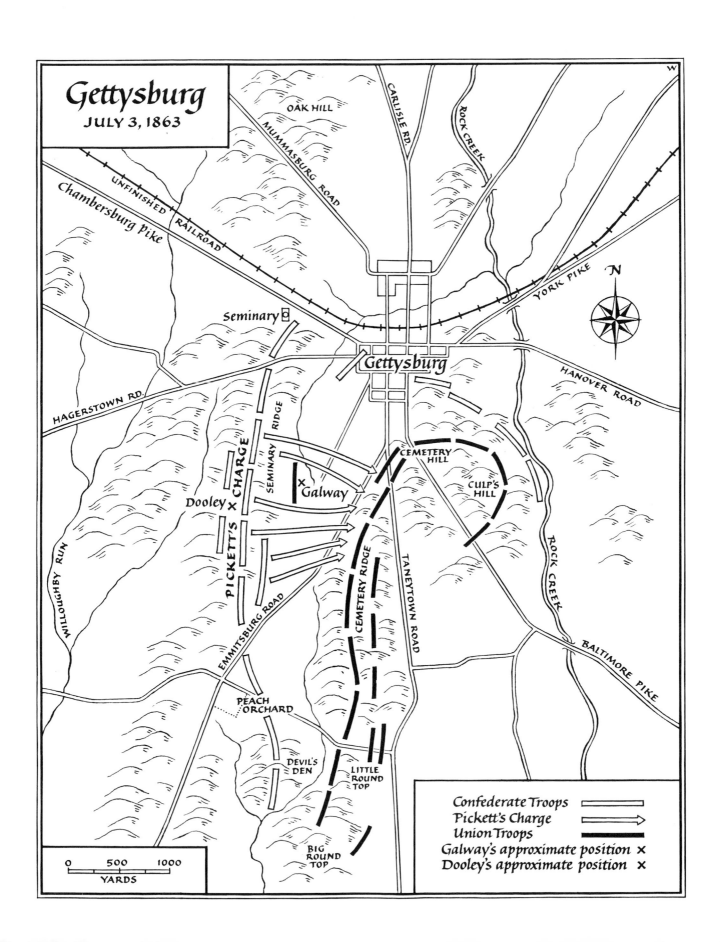

Gettysburg
JULY 3, 1863

W

OAK HILL

CARLISLE RD.

ROCK CREEK

MUMMASBURG ROAD

UNFINISHED RAILROAD

Chambersburg Pike

YORK PIKE

N

Seminary

Gettysburg

HANOVER ROAD

HAGERSTOWN RD.

SEMINARY RIDGE

CEMETERY HILL

CULP'S HILL

Galway

Dooley

PICKETT'S CHARGE

ROCK CREEK

WILLOUGHBY RUN

EMMITSBURG ROAD

CEMETERY RIDGE

TANEYTOWN ROAD

BALTIMORE PIKE

PEACH ORCHARD

DEVIL'S DEN

LITTLE ROUND TOP

BIG ROUND TOP

Confederate Troops
Pickett's Charge
Union Troops
Galway's approximate position ✕
Dooley's approximate position ✕

0   500   1000
YARDS

Union cannon found Dooley's regiment almost immediately. Dooley would recall in horror what the opening minutes of the cannon duel were like. "In one of our Regts. alone the killed and wounded, even before going into the charge, amounted to 88 men; and men lay bleeding and gasping in the agonies of death all around, and we are unable to help them in the least. . . . Some companion would raise his head disfigured and unrecognizable, streaming with blood, or would stretch his full length, his limbs quivering in the pangs of death. Orders were to lie as closely as possible to the ground, and I like a good soldier never got closer to the earth than on the present occasion."

THOMAS GALWAY discovered that from his advanced position he had a good view of the action both in front of and behind him. "Now and again a shell would strike one of our battery ammunition chests, blowing it up with a tremendous detonation. Still our artillery kept at their work, giving out Indian yells whenever they saw that their shots had taken good effect." An hour later, however, the constant thudding of the cannons began to wear away Galway's energy and he lost interest in what was happening around him. "After a while so monotonous became the roar of the artillery that it produced drowsiness amongst us, and I went to sleep. . . . Most of my regiment did as I did."

AT THIS POINT the Confederate general in charge of the artillery fire sent a terse message to General Pickett. "If you are coming at all you must come immediately or I cannot give you proper support."

Pickett wanted his orders to come directly from Longstreet, so he did not order the charge.

The cannon fire went on for another ten minutes, then the general in charge of the artillery sent another note to Pickett: "For God's sake come quick!"

Pickett galloped over to Longstreet, showed him the message and asked, "General, shall I advance?"

An officer nearby describes what happened next. "General L. read the note and . . . turned around in his saddle and would not answer. Pickett immediately saluted, and said: 'I am going to lead my division forward, sir.' and gallopped off to put it in motion; on which General L. left his staff and rode out alone."

Pickett dashed back to where his men waited, hastily issuing orders to prepare for the charge. But it was already too late. Confederate artillery were desperately low on ammunition and would be able to continue the cannon barrage for only a few more minutes.

"The ammunition wagons fly back and forth bringing fresh supplies of ammunition," John Dooley noticed over an hour after the cannonade had started, "and still the air is shaking from earth to sky with every missile of death fired from the cannon's mouth. Around, above, beneath, and on all sides they screech, sing, scream, whistle, roar, whirr, buzz, bang and whizz, and we are obliged to lie quietly tho' frightened out of our wits."

Then the orders were shouted up and down the line. Dooley pushed himself up from the safety of his cover and began urging his men forward. After a moment's hesitation, the men responded and began moving forward, through the cloud of smoke. Ordinarily, Confederate cannon fire would continue to pound away at the Union line to provide cover for their troops while they crossed the open field. But the delay in ordering the charge had thrown off the timing in a fatal way. At the very moment Dooley and his men stepped into the open, Confederate artillery crews were loading the last of their shells.

THOMAS GALWAY awoke from his battlefield snooze with booming cannon fire ringing in his ears. When he looked around, he discovered that cannon smoke had settled over the field. He could barely make out the shapes of the men near him. "Shortly afterwards," he recalled, "I was struck in the foot by a spent shell fragment. After recovering from the pain of the impact, and whilst laughing at the matter, I was slapped in the thigh by a fragment of an enemy shell. This knocked me over, but I managed to pick myself up."

Suddenly, the cannon fire from the Confederate side lessened and then stopped. A few moments later, the Union artillery paused in its firing too. Another eerie quiet took hold of the battlefield and Galway strained to see through the acrid wall of smoke. "Then came a distant murmur from the front," Galway wrote. The smoke thinned and he could see shapes moving. "All at once the murmur increased into a prolonged yell, and we saw the enemy with colors advancing in columns in mass."

"Here they are," was shouted up and down the Union lines. "Here comes the infantry."

As the smoke lifted, fifteen thousand Confederate soldiers could be seen marching forward shoulder to shoulder in a column one and a half miles wide. Even though this was his enemy coming toward him, Galway was awed enough by what he saw to later recall: "I had often read of battles and of charges, but until this moment I had not gazed upon so grand a sight as was presented by that beautiful mass of gray, as it came on, cheering their peculiar cheer, right towards the crest of the hill which we and our batteries were to defend."

Galway soon came to his senses, hobbled to the fence just ahead of him and began firing at the Rebels closest to him. Union artillery opened up, too, lobbing a deadly rain of metal onto the column. Shells ripped up the earth in giant clots, sometimes killing ten men

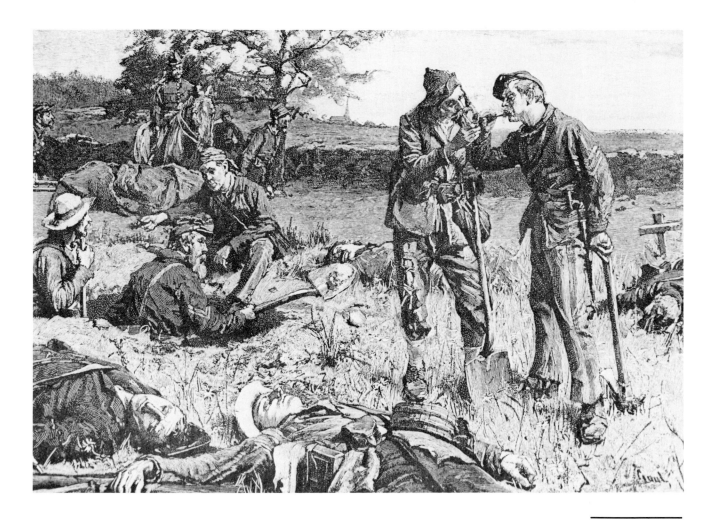

Confederate and
Union soldiers
put aside their
rifles for a short
time in order to
bury the dead.

at a time. One hundred pound cannon balls could be seen bouncing along the field headed directly into the Confederate line. Already, the Rebel line seemed ragged and uneven as hundreds of men fell, the lucky ones dead, the others alive but horribly mutilated.

"I TELL YOU," Dooley would say later, "there is no romance in making one of these charges. When you rise to your feet, I tell you the enthusiasm of ardent breasts in many cases *ain't there*. Instead of burning to avenge the insults of our country, families and altars

This Union drummer was lucky enough to survive Gettysburg.

and firesides, the thought is most frequently, Oh, if I could just come out of this charge safely how thankful would I be!"

STILL THOUSANDS of gray uniforms came forward and the barrel of Galway's rifle grew hot to the touch from the repeated firings. "We now heard the fearful din of our artillery," Galway wrote, "the savage, threatening yells of the advancing and now seemingly invincible enemy. . . . We stood all alone out in the open field."

For some reason, the Confederate line never bothered to attack Galway's company even though they would have been easy enough to overrun. Happily for Galway, the advancing column of enemy soldiers wheeled to the right and made themselves very easy targets.

"The enemy column has now approached the turnpike just to the south of us. . . ." Galway continued. "Still brave and cheering, they ascend the stone wall. Our men up there break and disappear

Even this rough sketch gives a good sense of the smoky chaos that accompanied the artillery duel on July 3.

beyond the crest of the ridge [and] for a few seconds things look dubious; the enemy has taken Griffin's battery and are about to train its guns on our own line."

SEVERAL DOZEN Confederate soldiers had survived the charge. They battled their way up the hill and actually took a section of the ridge not far from the clump of trees.

Dooley managed to cross the Emmitsburg road and lead his men halfway up the hill. "On! men, on!" Dooley shouted. "Thirty more yards and the guns are ours." But Union soldiers far outnumbered their forces and Dooley had to admit the obvious. "Who can stand such a storm of hissing lead and iron? Our men are falling faster now, for the deadly musket is at work. Volley after volley of crashing musket balls sweep through the line and mow us down like wheat before the scythe."

Dooley was less than one hundred feet from the enemy line when a musket ball struck him. "Shot through both thighs, I fall about 30 yards from the guns. By my side lies Lt. Kehoe, shot through the knee. Here we lie, he in excessive pain, I fearing to bleed to death, the dead and dying all around, while the division

Confederate soldiers duck behind anything available as shells scream and explode all around them.

sweeps over the Yankee guns. . . . We seem to have victory in our hands."

Just then Dooley heard a shout. "Cheer after cheer rends the air. Are those fresh troops advancing to our support?" he asked hopefully. Dooley's hope would soon be crushed. Hundreds of fed-

The landscape swarms with soldiers in the Union view of Pickett's Charge.

eral troops were rushing to the area, while nearby Union artillery continued to destroy the remaining Confederate troops. Few Confederate soldiers would make it up the hill to reinforce the position.

FROM HIS SPOT below the ridge, Galway recorded what happened. "Then in the nick of time Major Rorty . . . rallying a portion of the 29th New York, charges them and recovers the battery. The enemy, now broken and disorganized and far from support, begin to retire. The retreat is, almost at once, turned into a flight! They throw away everything — cartridge boxes, waistbelts, and haversacks — in their stampede. As far as the eye could reach, the ground was covered with flying Confederates."

Despite a severely bruised thigh, Galway managed to get to his feet, fix his bayonet to his rifle, and chase after the enemy. The fight was out of most of them, he remembered. Before the afternoon was

The two armies meet and fight at close quarters. The Union forces (on the left) would eventually push the enemy off the hill.

over, he was able to round up and bring in fifty prisoners without any help.

At around four o'clock, General Meade rode to the top of the ridge to see how the fight was going. The battlefield was still noisy and chaotic, so Meade had no clear idea of what was taking place. When he came upon an officer accompanying prisoners toward the rear, he asked, "How is it going?"

"I believe, General," came the reply, "the enemy's attack is repulsed."

"What! Is the assault already repulsed?"

"It is, sir."

Again, Meade scanned the scene — gray uniforms scurrying away in retreat, the dead on the field, Union soldiers rounding up prisoners, the wounded all around, begging for help. Then he muttered, half to himself, "Thank God."

A MILE AWAY, General Lee moved among his retreating soldiers and tried to encourage them. "It is all my fault," he told them. "All this will come right in the end, but in the meantime, all good men must rally." Most of the Confederate soldiers, even those badly wounded, took off their hats and cheered him.

Lee tried to be rational about what had happened that day. He told one of his officers, "This has been a sad day for us, a sad day; but we can't expect always to gain victories." But he could not ignore the streams of soldiers limping past him, or the reports that were coming to him about the number of wounded and dead. He had suffered a terrible defeat and he knew it. Finally, the emotions he'd hidden broke through, and he cried out, "Oh, too bad! Too bad!"

Because of his injuries, Dooley was not a part of the Confederate retreat. He lay on the ridge, bleeding, all during the hot afternoon and into the humid darkness of night. They had broken through the center of the Union line and come close to victory. So very close. His one thought during much of this time: "But for a little well timed support and Gettysburg was ours."

Union reinforcements move in to secure Cemetery Hill.

As Confederate troops withdrew, their artillery tried to hold off the Union forces. The large puff of smoke at the left is where a shell exploded, killing Sergeant Edward Duffey. He would be the last Confederate soldier to die at Gettysburg.

Three Confederate soldiers, unhappy prisoners.

6

A FEW APPROPRIATE REMARKS

---

*T*HOMAS Galway handed his prisoners over to a detail of soldiers, then watched as the last of the retreating Confederate soldiers disappeared into the trees. The shooting lessened, then stopped, and an exhausted Galway turned to study the battlefield. Fires burned in many places of the field, fences and tree trunks were splintered, wagons overturned and shattered like so many toys. And all around him were the dead and wounded.

"When we had reached the ditch of the Emmitsburg Pike on our way back, we beheld a sorry sight. Many of the wounded had been carried back to it during the fight. Others had hobbled and crawled into it, some dying after reaching it. It was full of pools of blood, and the grass for some distance in front was saturated with blood. In the ditch along with many others in like condition, lay two of our sergeants, Fairchild and Kelly; each with the lower part of the leg hanging by a piece of flesh to the rest of the limb."

Ambulances moved over the battlefield, while soldiers searched through the piles of bodies for friends who might still be alive. In all, over six thousand men died in the three days of fighting and almost forty-two thousand were wounded. "The whole ground around us is a great hospital," Galway recalled. "Every house, every barn, was made into a hospital. Men ran everywhere seeking wounded comrades."

The task was too huge for the tired soldiers and soon darkness made it difficult to search the torn-up field. Late that night, a steady rain added to the difficulty of helping the wounded. "Night came on," Galway says, "and then the only sound to be heard were the groans of the wounded, the prayers of the dying, and the strident noises of shelter tents and clothes of all sorts being torn up for bandages. After doing all I could for such of my own wounded as I could find, I lay down and slept."

While their comrades flee south, these Confederate soldiers are being marched off to prison in the North.

LIKE MANY of the other wounded, John Dooley spent the night unattended. "I have slept a little despite a steady but light fall of rain which has undoubtedly proved refreshing to thousands of fevered brains and burning wounds." A few hours after dawn on the 4th of July, an ambulance crew finally spotted Dooley and took him to the nearest hospital.

"The rain is pouring down as we reach the field hospital, which differs from the battle field only in this respect, that we have some kind of medical attendance and rations of crackers and substitute-coffee. But the accommodations are the same, [that is] the wet muddy hillside, [without] tents, blankets, fires, or water."

Surgeons worked feverishly, mostly amputating mangled arms and legs. Those, like Dooley, who appeared to be in no immediate danger of death had to wait. One of Dooley's men sat nearby,

Union and Confederate dead were separated and then lined up for burial. Confederate soldiers, like these, were usually buried last.

seemingly uninjured. When Dooley asked him what was the matter, "He opens his shirt and quietly points to a piece of shell which is half buried in the hollow between his breasts. He tells me . . . that he feels his time has come and that no one will by proper care give him a chance, if there be any chance, to recover from his wound."

Dooley passed another day and a night in the open. "This is a horrid night, cold and wet and rainy," he noted sadly. "Groans and shrieks and maniacal ravings; bitter sobs, and heavy sighs, piteous cries; horrid oaths; despair; the death rattle; darkness; death. . . . All night long I lie awake shivering with cold save when my wearied eye lids droop for a moment, again to be opened by a convulsive start as the wheels of the ambulance all but run over my feet, bringing more and more from the field of blood."

Three days after the fighting at Gettysburg ended, Dooley was

Bodies left exposed in the fields around Gettysburg were a common sight for weeks after the battle.

Meade used this little stone farmhouse as his headquarters. Three days of shelling shattered the fences and walls, ripped up the orchard, and left dead horses in the road.

moved to a tent hospital where his wounds were treated. Because they had run out of most supplies, all the doctors could do was wash and pour whiskey over his wounds and then wrap them with pieces of a torn shirt. The next day Dooley was put in a wagon loaded with other Confederate wounded and made a bumpy and painful trip north to a Union prison.

THOMAS GALWAY spent July 4 on a burial detail. "The corpses are brought into rows and counted, the Confederates and Federals being separated into different rows. At the feet of each row of fifty or a hundred dead, a trench is dug about seven feet wide and about three feet deep — for there is not time for a normal grave depth. Then the bodies, which are as black as ink and bloated from exposure to the sun, are placed in the shallow ditch and quickly covered with dirt."

Newspaper reporters prowled the battlefield gathering stories of the fighting. Sketch artists and photographers began the task of documenting what had happened during the three-day battle. These were joined by droves of civilians. Galway was annoyed at the way civilians strolled around the battlefield, as if it were some sort of amusement park arranged for their pleasure. "Curiosity is their main motive in visiting the places where anything remarkable occurred during the battle, and to gaze with ludicrous horror at the black and mutilated dead who are strewn everywhere. . . . Already the souvenir hunters are scattered over the field, picking up relics of the battle. Cannon balls are especially sought for by these people."

The dead were hastily buried in shallow graves and marked in whatever way was possible. Here, planks ripped from a nearby barn serve as grave markers.

The smoke had barely cleared when visitors began arriving to see the torn-up battlefield and hunt for souvenirs.

At some point in the day, Galway took a break and climbed the slope to Cemetery Ridge. The trees around him were like skeletons, shot up and stripped of leaves. Below him, the once rolling countryside was scarred with craters and wreckage, men scurrying about like busy ants. He walked over to Cemetery Hill where the heaviest fighting had taken place. Near the gate, he spotted a little sign and chuckled when he read the words painted on it: "All persons found using firearms in these grounds will be prosecuted with the utmost rigor of the law."

On July 5, Galway's company received orders to rejoin the rest of the army as it pursued what was left of Lee's army. Meade would not press another major fight. He knew that his troops had spent weeks marching in the heat and had fought for three days with little rest or food. They were exhausted and he did not want to commit a blunder now that the Union army had the edge.

President Lincoln was encouraged when he received word of the Union victory at Gettysburg, but he was anxious that Meade not let Lee's army slip away. "Now if General Meade can complete his work," he is reported to have told a general at the War Department, "by the literal or substantial destruction of Lee's army, the rebellion will be over."

The rains made movement difficult, but Meade did get his troops reorganized and trailing the Confederate forces. He had no intention of charging them directly. He wanted to find out their exact strength before doing this, so he sent out cavalry to probe the enemy. They discovered that Lee was at the Potomac in a strong defensive position.

A thunderstorm was moving in and lightning flashed in the sky. A decision was made to postpone any attack until the next day when more information could be gathered on the enemy's strength.

This did not please Lincoln, who immediately had a telegram sent to Meade that said: "You are strong enough to attack and defeat the enemy before he can effect a crossing. . . . Do not let the enemy escape."

Meade was in no mood to be criticized, and he sent back a curt reply: "My Army is and has been making forced marches short of rations and barefooted. . . . [It] marched yesterday and last night 30 miles. I take occasion to repeat that I will use my utmost efforts to push forward this Army."

But when morning came, almost all of Lee's army had managed to cross the river on a hastily constructed bridge. When this news reached Lincoln, he was angry enough to grumble: "I could have whipped Lee myself."

It would be months before the magnitude of the Union victory could be appreciated. The Civil War was not over, of course, and would not be for another two years. But the South had lost one third of its army at Gettysburg and would never regain its full fighting force or threaten the North again. In addition, as time went by and people in the North realized how badly the Confederate army had been beaten, they began to support Lincoln more fully. When the 1864 presidential elections rolled around, Lincoln was reelected overwhelmingly.

Lincoln could not foresee these positive results. Even if he could, it probably would not have changed his mood. As far as Lincoln was concerned, the job was not over. He would make his daily trips to the War Department to read the telegrams and continue to urge his generals to attack until the South surrendered.

Too late. Union troops arrived at the Potomac, but Lee and his army were long gone.

As MEADE and his army moved away from Gettysburg, another group of people descended on the battlefield — members of the local cemetery association. They found themselves confronted with an overwhelming job.

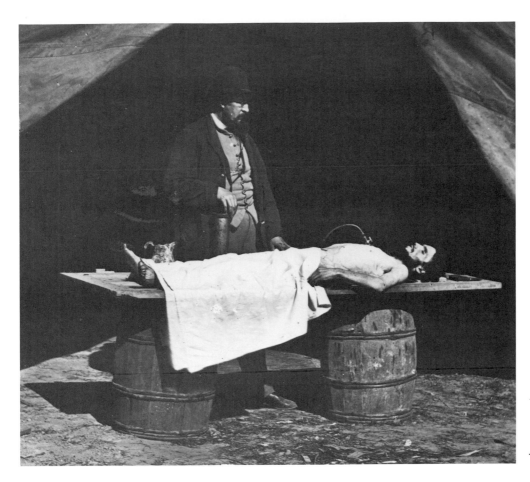

An embalmer at work in his crude battlefield facilities.

Hundreds of bodies were still exposed on the ridges and in the valley where they had fallen. Just days after the end of the fighting, the stench in the humid July weather was overpowering. Some of those who had been quickly buried in the fields around Gettysburg were even causing problems. As soon as possible after the conflict, farmers began ploughing in order to plant a late season crop of wheat. Unfortunately, it was difficult to tell where graves had been dug in the chewed up ground, so farmers often disinterred bodies by mistake. A resident of Gettysburg wrote that "arms and legs, and sometimes heads, protrude, and my attention has been directed to several places where hogs were actually rooting out bodies and devouring them."

The only real solution to the problem was to dig up all the bodies and give them proper burials. But who would pay for the land, wooden coffins, and grave markers? In the past, the federal government had left the chore and the costs of cleaning up after a battle to the local government, so no financial aid would be coming to Gettysburg. The local cemetery association had an answer. It would purchase a plot of land and ask the families of the dead soldiers to pay for their burial.

A Gettysburg resident, David Wills, heard about the scheme and objected. These soldiers had already paid the ultimate price for

Abraham Trostle's farm was in ruins, his field clogged with dead horses. It would be Trostle's responsibility to clean it all up and repair the damage.

their country, he argued. It was indecent to force their families pay again. He wrote to the governor of Pennsylvania and proposed that a National Soldiers Cemetery be established, with the costs being shared by all of the states in the Union. The governor agreed and Wills purchased sixteen acres of the battlefield for $2,475.87.

The work of removing and reburying the bodies began in October and took over a year to complete. At the same time, plans for a dedication ceremony were set in motion. Wills and the rest of the Cemetery Board immediately asked one of the nation's foremost speakers, Edward Everett, if he would deliver the dedication speech.

David Wills.

No one thought about asking President Lincoln to speak. In fact the Board didn't even think he would come to the ceremony — so it sent him an ordinary printed invitation, the same that was sent to hundreds of other people. Only when Lincoln said he would be there did the Board consider asking him to speak.

"The proposition to ask Mr. Lincoln to speak at Gettysburg was an afterthought," one member of the Board later confessed. "Scarcely any member of the Board, excepting the member from Illinois, had ever heard him speak at all . . . [and] the question was raised as to his ability to speak upon such a grave and solemn occasion."

The Board argued for several days and then, finally, on November 2, Wills sent a letter to Lincoln inviting him to "formally set apart these grounds to their sacred use by a few appropriate remarks."

While Lincoln jotted down ideas and phrases for his speech and Everett memorized his, work at the cemetery went on. The wreckage of the battlefield — shattered wagons and cannons, dis-

A sad, cold mist has settled over the ravaged field that was once lush countryside.

carded rifles, caps, spent shells, and the decaying remains of over fifteen hundred horses — was cleared away. The graves were arranged in neat arcs of a series of concentric circles, each topped with a bone white headstone. More and more headstones were added, sometimes as many as sixty in a day when the weather permitted. By the time November 19 arrived, an army of stone, silent and yet deeply eloquent, stood at attention to greet the people who came to Gettysburg.

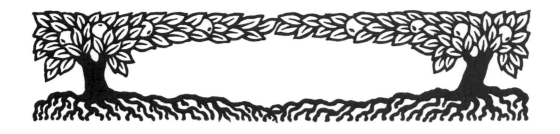

CONCLUSION

ONE hour and forty-five minutes after beginning, Edward Everett began to wind up his speech. Many in the crowd had grown restless and a few had even wandered off to explore the battlefield. Most of the listeners remained, eager to hear every word the great orator had to say.

Abraham Lincoln slipped his wire-rimmed glasses from a coat pocket and put them on. Next he unfolded the two pieces of paper on which he had written his speech to study it one last time.

Everett came to the final line of his oration: "But they, I am sure, will join us in saying as we bid farewell to the dust of these martyr-heroes, that wheresoever throughout the civilized world the accounts of this great warfare are read, and down to the latest period of recorded time, in the glorious annals of our common country there will be no brighter page than that which relates THE BATTLES OF GETTYSBURG."

Loud and enthusiastic applause followed Everett's speech and everyone agreed that his words had captured the solemn feeling of the occasion. After this, a hymn written especially for the dedication was played, followed by the introduction of Lincoln.

When Lincoln stood he was greeted with scattered applause from the weary audience. If the crowd's reception was lukewarm, the newspaper reviews of his speech would be icy cold. The major

The Gettysburg Address was so short that the photographer didn't have time to get a shot of Lincoln. Here the President can just be seen as he sits down.

newspapers printed his speech in full, but did not bother to comment on what he said. The Chicago *Times* ran a lengthy story about the ceremony, but only got around to mentioning Lincoln in the very last line: "President Lincoln made a few remarks upon the occasion."

Newspapers that did not support Lincoln or his policies usually had a great deal more to say. One, the *Patriot and Union,* of Harrisburg, Pennsylvania, had this comment: "We pass over the silly remarks of the President; for the credit of the nation we are willing that the veil of oblivion shall be dropped over them and that they shall no more be repeated or thought of."

Even Lincoln doubted that his speech had been a success. Moments after the ceremony concluded, Lincoln turned to his longtime friend, Ward Lamon, and said, "Lamon, that speech . . . is a flat failure and the people are disappointed."

But Lincoln's two-hundred-and-sixty-nine-word Gettysburg Address would be repeated and thought about a great deal. Its simple words and phrases spoke deeply about a country whose Constitution stated that "all men are created equal." It was an idea worth fighting and dying for, Lincoln was telling his listeners. The soldiers buried at Gettysburg had made the ultimate sacrifice. Now it was up to the living and all of their descendants to defend the principle of equality for *all*.

Lincoln waited a moment for the crowd to settle down and reminded himself to speak very slowly. Then, with a pronounced Kentucky accent, he said, "Four score and seven years ago our fathers brought forth on this continent a new nation conceived in liberty and dedicated to the proposition that all men are created equal.

"Now we are engaged in a great civil war testing whether that nation, or any nation so conceived and so dedicated, can long endure. We are met on a great battlefield of that war. We have come to dedicate a portion of that field as a final resting-place for those who here gave their lives that that nation might live. It is altogether fitting and proper that we should do this.

"But, in a larger sense, we can not dedicate, we can not consecrate, we can not hallow this ground. The brave men, living and dead, who struggled here have consecrated it far above our poor power to add or detract. The world will little note nor long remember what we say here, but it can never forget what they did here. It is for us the living rather to be dedicated here to the unfinished work which they who have fought here have so nobly advanced. It is rather for us to be here dedicated to the great task remaining before us — that from these honored dead we take increased devotion to that cause for which they here gave the last full measure of devotion — that we here highly resolve that these dead shall not have died in vain, that this nation under God shall have a new birth of freedom, and that government of the people, by the people, for the people shall not perish from the earth."

Four score and seven years ago our fathers brought forth, upon this continent, a new nation, conceived in Liberty, and dedicated to the proposition that all men are created equal.

Now we are engaged in a great civil war, testing whether that nation, or any nation, so conceived, and so dedicated, can long endure. We are met here on a great battle-field of that war. We have come to dedicate a portion of it, as a final resting place for those who here gave their lives, that that nation might live. It is altogether fitting and proper that we should do this.

But in a larger sense we can not dedicate— we can not consecrate— we can not hallow this ground. The brave men, living and dead, who struggled here, have consecrated it far above our poor power to add or detract. The world will little note, nor long remember, what we say here, but can never forget what they did here. It is for us, the living, rather to be dedicated here to the unfinished work which they have, thus far, so nobly carried on. It is rather

for us to be here dedicated to the great
task remaining before us,— that from these
honored dead we take increased devotion
to ~~the~~ that cause for which they here gave ~~gave~~
the last full measure of devotion— that
we here highly resolve that these dead
shall not have died in vain; that this
nation shall have a new birth of freedom;
and that this government of the people, by
the people, for the people, shall not perish
from the earth.

WHAT HAPPENED to John Dooley and Thomas Galway after Gettysburg was as different as the sides of the war they fought on. After being taken from the Gettysburg battlefield, Dooley was shipped to Fort McHenry prison, a place not much better then the crude battlefield hospital where he was first treated. There were no beds or pillows or blankets for the wounded and food was so scarce that roasted rat became a treat.

No doctors attended Dooley's wounds and they soon grew infected. For several months, Dooley battled a high fever and terrible pain with only the help of fellow prisoners to change the dirty strips of cloth that were used as a bandage. Dooley would be one of the few prisoners to survive his wounds. Even so, he would spend another two years in McHenry before being released.

His return to his hometown of Richmond did not bring him any real joy. He found the city in ruins, buildings blasted into rubble, the roads torn up and useless. Worse, the city was crawling with Yankee soldiers.

In September 1865, Dooley entered the Novitiate of the Jesuit Order at Georgetown in order to become a priest. He would study for several years, and was known as a fine teacher of boys studying in the preparatory school of the college.

Unfortunately, Dooley's health, frail at the beginning of the war, had been damaged beyond repair by his wounds. He developed a lung condition in 1868 and had to spend many weeks in the infirmary. He died in May 1873, just nine months before he was to be ordained to the priesthood. For Dooley, his entire world and all of his dreams had been consumed by the Civil War.

By contrast, Thomas Galway seemed to lead a charmed life. He fought in a number of other major battles, but managed to escape serious injury. At the end of the conflict, he'd earned a number of medals for bravery and attained the rank of Brevet Captain, which means he functioned in the capacity of a captain, but had not received the official commission. Brevet Captain would be his nickname for life.

He returned to his hometown of Cleveland where he married and attended college to become an engineer and a lawyer. Instead of putting either degree to use when he graduated, Galway and his wife moved to New York City. There they raised four children while he demonstrated another of his talents. Galway spoke seven or eight languages fluently, so he became Professor of Logic and French Literature and Latin at Manhattan College, a position he held for over thirty-five years.

Galway maintained his energy and spirit and biting wit well into his seventies and was a noted and much loved character in his neighborhood. From time to time, however, his more serious side would surface. He condemned the hunting of deer as "sadistic" and worked for many years to expel the British from Ireland. His most noted cause had to do with racial integration.

Galway and his family lived in a well-to-do neighborhood in Harlem, a street then filled with large Victorian homes. A black family purchased a home next door to Galway's. Two brothers who lived in a gigantic house across the street objected and tried to have the family evicted. At the trial, Galway dusted off his lawyer's skills and defended the black family's right to live on the block. Galway won the case easily. Later, Galway's son, Geoffrey, would note, "He liked to thwart oppression . . . and made it clear that he had fought to free [blacks] and give them equal citizenship."

B I B L I O G R A P H Y

All information about John Dooley and Thomas Galway comes from their personal war journals. Both texts were published in the mid-1940s and are currently out of print.

Dooley, John. *John Dooley: Confederate Soldier: His War Journal*. Washington, DC: Georgetown University Press, 1945.

Galway, Thomas Francis. *The Valiant Hours*. Harrisburg, PA: Stackpole Co., 1946.

Details about Abraham Lincoln, the circumstances surrounding his Gettysburg Address, his dealings with his generals, and his military role in the Battle of Gettysburg come from a variety of sources. The following is a list of the most important.

Bates, David H. *Lincoln in the Telegraph Office*. New York, 1907.

Catton, Bruce. *Glory Road: The Bloody Route from Fredericksburg to Gettysburg*. Garden City, NY: Doubleday & Co., 1952.

———. *Mr. Lincoln's Army*. Garden City, NY: Doubleday & Co., 1951.

Cleaves, Freeman. *Meade of Gettysburg*. Norman, OK: University of Oklahoma Press, 1960.

Doubleday, Abner. *Chancellorsville and Gettysburg*. New York: Harper & Bros., 1882.

Freedman, Russell. *Lincoln: A Photobiography*. New York: Clarion Books, 1987.

Lamon, Ward Hill. *Recollections of Abraham Lincoln, 1847–1865*. Washington, DC: A.C. McClurg & Co., 1895.

Lincoln, Abraham. *Complete Works of Abraham Lincoln,* 12 vols. Ed. by John G. Nicolay and John Hay. New York: The Century Co., 1894.

Meade, George. *Life and Letters of George Gordon Meade,* 2 vols. New York: Charles Scribner's Sons, 1913.

Salles, Robert. *Lincoln at Gettysburg.* Washington, DC: Philip & Solomons, 1913.

Sandburg, Carl. *Abraham Lincoln: The War Years,* 4 vols. New York: Harcourt, Brace & Co., 1954.

Williams, T. Harry. *Lincoln and His Generals.* New York: Alfred A. Knopf, 1952.

Hundreds of books have been written about the Battle of Gettysburg and thousands more have been written about the Civil War in general. The following list contains many with photographs and illustrations of the soldiers, generals, and politicians involved in the conflict.

Alexander, E. P. *Military Memoirs of a Confederate.* New York: Charles Scribner's Sons, 1907.

Bellah, James Warner. *Soldiers' Battle: Gettysburg.* New York: David McKay Co., 1962.

Billings, John D. *Hardtack and Coffee, or, The Unwritten Story of Army Life.* Boston: George M. Smith & Co., 1887.

Catton, Bruce. *Never Call Retreat.* New York: Washington Square Press, 1965.

———. *This Hallowed Ground: The Story of the Union Side of the Civil War.* Garden City, NY: Doubleday & Co., 1956.

Commager, Henry Steele, ed. *The Blue and the Gray: The Story of the Civil War as Told by Participants: Volume Two: The Battle of Gettysburg to Appomattox.* Indianapolis: The Bobbs-Merrill Co., 1950.

Dowdey, Clifford. *The Land They Fought For: The Story of the South as the Confederacy, 1832–1865.* Garden City, NY: Doubleday & Co., 1955.

Editors of Century Magazine. *The Century War Book: The Famous History of the Civil War by the People Who Actually Fought.* New York: The Century Co., 1884.

Foote, Shelby. *The Civil War: A Narrative,* 3 vols. New York: Random House, 1958–1974.

Freeman, Douglas Southall. *Lee's Lieutenants,* 3 vols. New York: Charles Scribner's Sons, 1944.

Haskell, Frank A. *The Battle of Gettysburg.* Madison, WI: Wisconsin History Commission, 1908.

Hoke, Jacob. *Remembrances of the War.* Chambersburg, PA: M. A. Foltz, 1884.

Jacobs, M. *The Rebel Invasion of Maryland and Pennsylvania.* Philadelphia, PA: J. B. Lippincott Co., 1864.

Lossing, B. J. *A History of the Civil War.* New York: Harper & Sons, 1912.

McPherson, James M. *Battle Cry of Freedom: The Civil War Era.* New York: Oxford University Press, 1988.

Miller, Francis T., ed. *The Photographic History of the Civil War,* 10 vols. New York: Review of Reviews Co., 1912.

Mitchell, Joseph B. *Decisive Battles of the Civil War.* New York: G. P. Putnam's Sons, 1955.

Sanger, D. B., and Thomas R. Hay. *James Longstreet.* Baton Rouge, LA: Louisiana State University Press, 1952.

Truesdale, John. *The Blue Coats: How They Lived, Fought and Died for the Union.* Philadelphia: Jones Brothers & Co., 1867.

Toombs, Samuel. *New Jersey Troops in the Gettysburg Campaign.* Orange, NJ: Evening Mail Publishing House, 1888.

INDEX

Italic type indicates illustrations